Russian Cuisine in Exile

Russian Cuisine in Exile

PYOTR VAIL and ALEXANDER GENIS

Authorized translation by
ANGELA BRINTLINGER and THOMAS FEERICK

Boston
2018

Library of Congress Cataloging-in-Publication Data

Names: Vail', Petr, 1949–2009, author. | Genis, Alexander, author. | Brintlinger, Angela, translator. | Feerick, Thomas, translator.

Title: Russian cuisine in exile/Petr Vail and Alexander Genis (1987); authorized translation by Angela Brintlinger and Thomas Feerick.

Other titles: Russkaia kukhnia v izgnanii. English

Description: Brighton, MA: Academic Studies Press, 2018. | Translation of: Russkaia kukhnia v izgnanii Los Angeles. | Includes bibliographical references and index.

Identifiers: LCCN 2018023252 (print) | LCCN 2018025263 (ebook) | ISBN 9781618117311 (ebook) | ISBN 9781618117304 (pbk.: alk. paper)

Subjects: LCSH: Cooking, Russian. | Cooking.

Classification: LCC TX723.3 (ebook) | LCC TX723.3 .V3513 2018 (print) | DDC 641.5947—dc23

LC record available at https://lccn.loc.gov/2018023252

Book design by Kryon Publishing Services Pvt. Ltd.
http://www.kryonpublishing.com

Cover design by Ivan Grave

Published by Academic Studies Press in 2018
28 Montfern Avenue
Brighton, MA 02135, USA
press@academicstudiespress.com
www.academicstudiespress.com

Table of Contents

Acknowledgments

In spring 2016 my students were looking for a task worthy of their final semester as Russian majors, and we decided to tackle *Russian Cuisine in Exile* together. Thanks go to Christian Brymer, Zhanna Kaganovich, Ayleen Keeton, Chris Kuzak, Heather Long, DeAnna Miller and Becca Morford for giving us permission to work with their draft translations of seven of the chapters in this book. Of these talented students, Thomas Feerick turned out to be the most intrepid of all. Starting with chapter 16, Mushroom Metaphysics, he entered into the endeavor with gusto, and though the task did not make a mushroom lover out of him, he came on board as my co-translator of the book anyway. His insights have been impressive, and his tenacity worthy of emulation. It has been a great partnership.

We owe a debt of gratitude to Faith Stein, who enthusiastically endorsed the idea of publishing this translation, and to the detail-oriented eye of our copy-editor, Candace McNulty. Ivan Grave and the specialists of Kryon Publishing have been brilliant with design and layout, and the book has benefited from Kira Nemirovsky's care and thoughtfulness. The Ohio State University College of Arts and Sciences awarded us a grant to obtain the translation rights, and Alexander Genis, along with Pyotr Vail's widow Elya, graciously agreed to our project. We thank Alexander Genis for his helpful input on the text and commentaries and for the terrific interview found at the end of the book.

Thanks as always to Steve Conn and Olivia and Zack Brintlinger-Conn, for their tolerance and good humor with this and all my crazy projects, and to Ohio State for the sabbatical leave during 2016–17 that enabled me to complete the book.

Angela Brintlinger
Yellow Springs, Ohio
June 2017

My eternal thanks to my family: Patricia, John Jr., Meaghan, and Catherine Feerick, for exposing me to a thousand funny things that informed the humor I've tried to bring to this project and being generally excellent people.

The gratitude I have left goes to the excellent instructors I've had, including my co-translator, whose generosity and enthusiasm make light work of any task. Special mention is also owed to Madame Catherine LaPlante for lighting a candle, and Marina Alexeevna Pashkova for setting it on a lake of gasoline.

Thomas Feerick
Columbus, Ohio
June 2017

Preface

In today's gastronomically obsessed landscape, with chefs competing on television, cuisine blogs proliferating on the internet, food selfies on Facebook, and Julia Child's entire kitchen firmly ensconced at the Smithsonian, this fact seems obvious: Food is culture.

But the 1970s in the United States were not a time of great cuisine. (I know—I still have my great aunt's recipe box from 1975. Canned soup, corn flakes, and marshmallows feature in an alarming percentage of recipes.) When Pyotr Vail (the "yo" in **Pyo**tr is pronounced much as you might hear "YO!" on the streets of New York) and Alexander Genis emigrated from the Soviet Union in 1977, they were surprised at how much they missed the cuisine they had known since childhood, and they were horrified by much of what they found here. The whitest of white breads, priorities of convenience over taste, food whose primary virtue was the speed with which it arrived. They did not really understand American culture, but what they perceived made them long for the habits of their homeland.

After arriving in the United States, Vail and Genis began to work in both newspaper and radio in New York City (among other things writing and presenting stories on the Russian Service of Radio Liberty). They were part of a larger community of writers and artists, including Vagrich Bakhchinyan, Lev Loseff, Joseph Brodsky, and Sergei Dovlatov, with whom they founded the short-lived weekly newspaper *Novyi Amerikanets* (*New American*). What made these émigrés into a true community was their shared level of sophistication and their encoded language of humor and satire, and Vail and Genis wrote with them and for them. A cross-section of Soviet dissident society, brought together primarily from the capitals of Moscow and Leningrad, but repeating the multiethnic nature of their country of origin, these émigrés were Jews, Armenians, Georgians, Russians, often in combination, and their food culture drew on that history.

Vail and Genis were actually from Latvia, but they quickly embraced the New York area as their home. Until 1990 they wrote together, as a team, and their output included such books as *The Sixties: The Soviet People's World* and *Native Tongue*, both of which remain in print today.[1] The authors "separated" after 1990 and continued their own careers. Genis remained in the U.S. while Vail decamped for Europe, where he reported on events including the first war in Chechnya. When the headquarters of Radio Liberty's Russia service moved to Prague in 1995, Vail became managing editor there. He died in that city in 2009 after a long illness.

By leaving the Soviet Union, Vail and Genis joined a larger Russian diaspora, what has been called Russia Abroad or the "Russian emigration" (as though that were a place, not a description), participating in the so-called "third wave" of Russian emigration after 1917.[2] After the Revolution over a million Russians—the "white émigrés" or first wave of emigration—fled the Bolsheviks. Most went to Europe, though some ended up in Harbin and Shanghai, China, and a few even landed in New York. The "second wave" included secondary émigrés, as refugees in Europe moved on to the UK or United States, as well as those who fled the Soviet Union during and after World War II.

Gleb Struve was one of those itinerant émigrés who left Russia after the Revolution. From Paris to London to Berkeley, he spent several decades moving house, only to establish himself eventually at the University of California. From there he wrote his *Russian Literature in Exile* (1956).[3] His choice of vocabulary—not émigré literature, not diaspora literature, but literature that has been driven out of its homeland, cast out, banished, ostracized—reflected the spirit of his enterprise. None of the literary figures he wrote about, or so Struve implied, left their homeland of their own free will. Instead they had been expelled, and their mission in exile was to maintain, protect, and nurture their national literature, in order to be ready at any moment to return home and take up pride of place in Russia again. That didn't happen, of course, until the 1990s.

---

[1] *60-e: Mir sovetskogo cheloveka* (Ann Arbor, MI: Ardis, 1988) and *Rodnaia rech'* (Tenafly, NJ: Hermitage, 1990).

[2] For an encyclopedia of the emigration, see John Glad, *Russia Abroad*.

[3] For V&G's joke on this account, see note on *Russian Sex in Exile* in chapter 12. *Russkaia literatura v izgnanii* was published by the Chekhov publishing house in New York and YMCA Press in Paris.

When Vail and Genis wrote their book there was still no going home. But by pairing "cuisine" and "exile," Vail and Genis spoofed Struve's somewhat more melancholy project. Yes, we have had to leave our homeland, they seem to be saying, but let's have a little fun in our new environment. Soviet dissident culture of the 1970s and 1980s is characterized by the tone that pervades this book: satirical and yet gentle, affirming and at the same time bitter, hilariously deadpan and vividly poignant. And, I might add, quite difficult to translate.

We have striven mightily to capture that sensibility in this translation. When Alexander Genis looked over our work he wrote, "I rejoiced every time I saw that you were translating not word for word but smile for smile, as Dovlatov used to beg his translators to do." We were delighted too with that response. And while it would be possible to simply present an English version of *Russian Cuisine in Exile* with no explanations at all, that seemed irresponsible. Instead we have supplied an extensive set of commentaries. At first Genis was put off. "I was horrified to see over two hundred notes," Genis said, "but then I realized that this was in itself a kind of game, a serious one that will allow Slavists and other crazy people to immerse themselves in culturological research."[4] That is exactly our goal.

Vail and Genis's book demonstrates a yearning for the time of their youth, when loose tea had not yet been sacrificed to the rapid convenience of teabags and processed cheese was a favorite chaser for a bout of drinking. Yet even as it functions in an *à la recherche de la cuisine perdue* way, with its self-deprecating humor, self-mockery, and all the plays on words, it refuses to take nostalgia too seriously. It is a cultural artifact of a time, and a place, and most importantly an attitude.

Like *Russian Literature in Exile*, with which *Russian Cuisine in Exile* surely resonates, this book documents and organizes historical material, in particular habits, preferences, and memories of the Soviet kitchen. (In fact, the title in English could easily be *The Russian Kitchen in Exile*—we think about Dovlatov's book of short stories, *The Suitcase*, in which each item he brought with him receives its history and backstory. Here the entire kitchen is unfolded in a New York apartment.) And like the peripatetic Struve, Vail, Genis, and other third wave émigrés made stops in Europe on the way to North America, which is why the Spanish paella and other recipes and ingredients unknown in the Soviet Union make it into the book.[5]

Importantly, this book is not a cookbook, not merely a reference book to check how to make borscht or *ukha* (fish soup), but a repository of a vanishing culture, a means of protecting and sharing that culture. It is also a record of a particular attitude, perhaps unique to dissidents or to émigrés—we loved our country, and we hated it, and the best way to explore and process those feelings is through humor. And finally, it *is* a recipe book. Pull a copy down off the shelf of any émigré and it will open magically to favorite dishes. *Russian Cuisine in Exile* was read, and it was used, by Russian émigrés across the world.

Ethnic restaurants have always sprung up in immigrant communities in the United States—consider Philadelphia's Italian South Philly or the Chinatowns of New York and San Francisco, or Greektown in Chicago. When we think of Russian cuisine in the United States today we usually imagine Brighton Beach, Brooklyn. Some in that wave of Soviet émigrés to which Vail and Genis belong were among the founders of those very restaurants and shops.

At the same time, Soviet cooking was home cooking, not restaurant fare—and émigrés needed help to remember the dishes they were used to and to figure out how to prepare them in their new consumer landscape. Russian-language newspapers were one of the ways that the far-flung Russian diaspora communicated with each other—the literary version of Little Odessa. Each place had its own paper, or even competing papers, and writers published wherever they could. When a fellow émigré suggested the column title "Russian Cuisine in Exile" for the Los Angeles newspaper *Panorama*, Vail and Genis were in business.

As they thought about food and culture, Vail and Genis quickly came to understand that their own mutual palate was formed from a completely unusual menu. One part nostalgia for Soviet canned goods and public catering options, one part Jewish tradition, one part cosmopolitanism that extended to the

---

[4] Genis compared our effort to the "Literary Monuments" series published by the Soviet and then Russian Academy of Sciences beginning in 1948 that presents the world's "great books" with academic commentaries. He personally believes that there is no such thing as too much commentary. We hope you will agree!

[5] As Masha Gessen explains, by the time in the early 1970s that the Soviet Union finally granted Soviet Jews the right to leave—hard-fought and won by Soviet Zionists—"the Soviet Union had long severed diplomatic ties with Israel. This meant, among other things, that a plane could not go directly from the Soviet Union to Israel, and neither could the Jews." While in Vienna or Rome, non-Zionist Jews "broke ranks" and "declared their intention to seek asylum in the U.S.—or Canada, or Australia" (*Where the Jews Aren't*, 141). David Bezmozgis, another Latvian Jewish refugee from the Soviet Union, chronicled his family's decision to choose Canada in the novel *The Free World*. I myself, after giving a scholarly lecture at Middlebury College, was treated to a Spanish paella concocted from Vail and Genis's recipe—a dish prepared for me by Sergei Davydov, a Russian émigré born in Czechoslovakia [AKB].

spicy foods of the Caucasus, plus a generous serving of the adventurous spirit that had made them dissidents in the first place, that palate led them to brave the unknowns of emigration and prompted them to experiment in the kitchen. Food, they discovered, was a major part of who they were: the comfort of family recipes, the habitual products of Soviet everyday life, the Russian and Ukrainian and Jewish and Georgian and Siberian specialties that they had tasted throughout their childhoods and young adulthoods.

The audience for these newspaper columns, and eventually the book *Russian Cuisine in Exile*, was as cosmopolitan as the authors. These Russian readers in exile were political and cultural dissidents, often Jews, and their personal histories involved poverty and deprivation, making do, and creating what we now call work-arounds to the obstacles in their paths. They were cultured, literate, politically sophisticated, steeped in the Russian classics from literature to history to ballet. They were also in desperate need of laughter, and Vail and Genis were just the men to deliver it. Being savvy and smart creators as well as consumers of public taste, Vail and Genis recognized a literary niche when they saw one.

It was thirty years ago, in 1987, that thirty-eight-year-old Pyotr Vail and thirty-four-year-old Alexander Genis penned this book, and it has gone on to be reprinted many times in the post-Soviet era. Now a beloved cultural artifact in post-Soviet Russia and across the world, *Russian Cuisine in Exile* is being translated into English for the very first time.

In the notes to the chapters of this book, the reader will find that the translators begin to refer to Vail and Genis as V&G. We do this for several reasons. First, the style of this book is very personal. It will draw you in as it drew us, and you will begin to feel a relationship developing with the authors. We certainly did, and as with any friends, we groaned at some puns, found jokes or descriptions that had us chuckling for days, and others that left us flat. Vail and Genis came to feel like relatives, like our co-conspirators, as we worked on rendering their clever phrasing, their literary allusions, or their typically Russian aphorisms into comprehensible English. Thus we dubbed them V&G (and when we asked Alexander Genis if this offended him, he assured us that it did not).

(Here we might imagine a scene in which we sit down to a favorite Russian beverage, probably vodka, with accompanying *zakuski* [snacks]. We talk, we laugh, we tell stories, we become inebriated. At some juncture one of us—Thomas, or Alexander, or Pyotr, or even me [though I'm a woman, which carries different connotations in drinking culture]—says, seriously or in jest: "Do you respect me?" In some happy afterlife we may all still get together to have that drink.)

Another reason why Vail and Genis became V&G to us was that we could not tell them apart as we translated—they write as one. Sometimes it seemed as if we could discern a personal voice through the prose, but we could never be sure. Were they conversing? arguing? sparring? speaking with one accent? playing off each other? America has a tradition of pairs of comedians: Abbott and Costello, Laurel and Hardy, Burns and Allen, Cheech and Chong, Key and Peele, and their routines involve physical slapstick as well as linguistic humor. But in Russia it has been literature that teems with partnerships. Kozma Prutkov, Ilf and Petrov, the Strugatsky brothers—this satirical tradition of writing as partners was another thing V&G brought with them into exile.

For the translators of *Russian Cuisine in Exile*, who have ourselves worked as a team, correcting each other, making suggestions, arguing over what we called our "points of contention," the term of affection V&G reminds us of P&V, the husband and wife translation team of Richard Pevear and Larissa Volokhonsky. Though neither Thomas nor I is a native speaker of Russian, we brought to the project extensive experience in Russian language and culture (AKB), a strong background in British humor (TF), deep knowledge of intertextual references (AKB), fresh eyes and a poetic touch (TF). So while we are not yet ready to dub ourselves B&F, we have had immense fun working together to transfer this comedic duo's philosophical, insightful, and often highly amusing view of the intersection of Russian/Soviet life and the American cultural landscape. We hope you will enjoy the result.

Introduction: Expressions of the Soul[1]

When the Japanese make declarations of love, they place their hand not on their heart but on their belly. They are sure that the soul resides in the stomach. This is why they perform hara-kiri, to set the soul free—which is a rather torturous way to reassure yourself of your own metaphysical being.

A Westerner, when talking about spiritual matters, might thump himself on the chest. If he does, he might feel, in the breast pocket of his coat, a Parker pen, a handkerchief, or even a billfold.[2] He won't find his soul, though, which lies three buttons below. You can grow accustomed to any geographic distance: longitude, latitude, altitude. But the umbilical cord, which ties a man to his home, naturally connects to the stomach, not the heart. Hearts may differ across the world. But no one can dictate to the stomach. Try to explain to the stomach, for example, that avocados are for eating and not just for decoration.[3]

The threads that tie a man to his homeland are many and varied: a rich culture, a mighty people, a glorious history. But the strongest threads stretch from the homeland to the soul. That is to say, to the stomach. These are not mere threads but more like ropes, Manila ropes. You can argue about culture, ethnicity, and history until morning, but can there really be any controversy about dried fish?[4]

They say you can't bring your country with you on the soles of your boots,[5] but you can bring crabs from the Far East, spicy Tallinn anchovies, store-bought layered

---

[1] The original Russian, *Dushi prekrasnye poryvy*, is quoted from Pushkin's ode "To Chaadaev" (1818): "My friend, let us dedicate to our country the beautiful outpourings of the soul!" Pyotr Chaadaev was a member of the Tsar's bodyguard in the Napoleonic Wars. After his resignation, he wrote a number of "Philosophical Letters," which criticized Russian culture. Nicholas I declared him insane in 1836. This is thought to be the first use of a diagnosis of mental illness to discredit a critic of the government in Russia.

[2] This translation modifies the "white man"/Japanese contrast of the original; the importance lies in the exoticism of Japanese cultural markers such as hara-kiri. Russians are perhaps closer to the "East"; at any rate, they value the "soul" in a way that Westerners do not. The everyday details here are striking, and the Parker pen is important. In the authors' childhoods a ballpoint pen—especially one that wrote smoothly—would have been a luxury. However, does anyone actually carry a billfold in his breast pocket?

[3] An avocado was quite an exotic food in the Soviet Union, one that must have seemed utterly improbable to new émigrés to America.

[4] Dried fish, *vobla*, here evokes Russian drinking parties where beer is the preferred accompaniment to this appetizer. Russians are tied together by their eating and drinking habits, and differing opinions about other matters pale in comparison to solidarity on this front.

[5] This expression, attributed to French revolutionary Georges Danton (1759–94), dates to the late eighteenth century, considerably before today's border control concerns about whether visitors have been on a farm or in a pasture while abroad.

wafer cakes, "Bears of the North" chocolates, and bottles of Essentuki artesian mineral water (the best is No. 17). A shopping list like this (plus hearty Russian mustard) makes living in an alien land (ooh, and unrefined sunflower oil) better (don't forget those tangy little tomatoes) and more joyful (and round it out with some six-star Ararat cognac).[6]

Of course, even with a spread like this there will still be room at the table for nostalgic memories. Suddenly, with a puff of pink smoke, out swims an aspic costing 36 kopeks, then piroshki with "jam," then "borscht b/m" (b/m means *bez miasa*, without meat, nothing indecent).[7] Also—hot greasy meat patties, bloody roast beef, Strasbourg pie. However, pardon, we've moved from nostalgia straight to the classics.[8] As the prophet of our own scandalous generation, Venichka Erofeev, said, "We are given only one life, and it's necessary to live it so as not to make mistakes in recipes."[9]

Our recipes, naturally, are not taken from the *Larousse Gastronomique* culinary encyclopedia,[10] but they do have one undeniable advantage: they are ours, assembled by the collective mind of the masses and imbued with the spirit of the nation. Can we really leave all that behind?[11] There will always be vegetarians and atheists who assert that the soul does not exist.[12] But, then, why should we bother with people for whom nothing is sacred?

---

[6] This sounds like a conversation between the two authors—one, trying to stay on topic, while the other keeps adding more items to the imagined shopping list. "Better and more joyful" evokes the Stalinist maxim: "Life has become better, comrades, life has become more joyful." The juxtaposition of this Stalinist phrase associated with multiethnic bounty (as advertised and promoted, for example, in the 1939 *Book of Healthy and Tasty Food*) onto the émigré's life "in an alien land" makes a good introduction to this book of recipes and essays—nostalgic, but always playful. The shopping list features the flavors of a pan-Soviet diet: Essentuki is in Southern Russia, near the Caucasus mountains, but Ararat cognac comes from Armenia. "Northern" chocolates, far Eastern crabs, and Estonian anchovies mean this list contains every point of the compass across the vast Soviet empire.

[7] As part of medical testing during the resettlement process, Russians—like all immigrants to the United States—were subjected to conversations with doctors and interpreters about b.m. (bowel movements). My own experience explaining about taking samples "*cherez stul*" (or every other b.m.) led to embarrassment and hilarity in sparsely furnished refugee apartments in the late 1980s. Among other things the Russian translation, *cherez stul*, sounded like I was asking the refugees to jump over kitchen chairs [AKB].

[8] These first items are all "proletarian" or everyday items one might find in a Soviet factory or school cafeteria, whereas the last two, "bloody roast beef" and "Strasbourg pie," are upper-class food items from Alexander Pushkin's 1820s novel-in-verse *Eugene Onegin*. Russians of the late Soviet period would know these lines, both because of the culturally conditioned habit of learning vast stretches of Pushkin's novel by heart, and because these dishes were so exotic as to be unattainable and even unimaginable in the Soviet era. We can see the logic as the "hot, greasy meat patties" lead directly into the "bloody roast beef"—but for a Russian reader, the other (also unattainable in the Soviet era) items on Pushkin's dinner menu would also be hovering in his mental background as he read: truffles, pineapple, Limburger cheese. See *Eugene Onegin*, chapter 1, verse XVI.

[9] The transition directly from the "poet-prophet" of the nineteenth century into the underground "prophet" of Soviet dissident culture indicates that the reader should take Venedikt Erofeev's alcohol-infused 1969 novel *Moscow to the End of the Line* (sometimes translated as *Moscow's Stations*) seriously as a vital cultural text. This quote from Erofeev's novel is a parody of another famous line from Nikolai Ostrovskii's classic Socialist Realist novel *How the Steel Was Tempered* (1936), spoken by his protagonist Pavel Korchagin: "We are given only one life, and it's necessary to live it so as not to feel excruciating pain about aimlessly lived years, so as not to feel burning shame about a miserable and trivial past and so that, dying, we can say: All my life and all my strength were devoted to the most wonderful thing in the world—the struggle to free mankind." The Pavel Korchagin line was memorized by all Soviet schoolchildren and was supposed to serve as a moral guide to how they lived their lives; Erofeev's line gives them a different message, a suggestion that they drink heavily, concocting more and more new and cheaper cocktails, which would help to obliterate the effects of official propaganda all around them.

[10] Both an important culinary artifact and, again, something very exotic to the Russian ear. The *Larousse* might evoke *à la russe* to someone unfamiliar with the name, but the next word in French, *gastronomique*, makes it clear that the homonym is only a coincidence.

[11] The "collective mind of the masses" and the "spirit of the nation" are Soviet clichés, but the authors' reluctance to part with them underscores the degree to which Soviet culture remained essential to those who chose to emigrate. And, of course, like many of V&G's borrowed expressions, these clichés drip with irony in their new usage.

[12] The "b/m" [without meat] in the previous paragraph indicates a cheaper soup for a student budget, although its precedent would have been a "fasting" version of beet soup for those who followed Russian Orthodox dietary restrictions. In the Soviet context, diners could not admit to following a religious diet, and yet vegetarianism for V&G is, as we see here, an abomination. So where does religious feeling inhere? Clearly for V&G, it is to be found in cuisine.

The Clay Pot—
A Repository of Tradition

If you like to eat, if you feel a natural nostalgia for the culinary relics of the homeland you left behind, if its traditions are dear to you—buy a clay pot. A capacious glazed clay pot with a tightly fitting lid—now that's a thing worth having! All of Russian cuisine comes out of it, the way that all Russian writers came out from under Gogol's overcoat.[1]

Technological progress has led to the invention of aluminum pots. But your life will be even better if you acquire this simple object, a gift from your ancient kin, who knew that the thick walls of a clay pot heat up slowly and evenly.

In the clay pot food does not boil, but rather stews. It retains all its vitamins, proteins, or whatever. (A normal person shouldn't worry about this. One doesn't thrive on vitamins, but on meat, fish, and vegetables.)

The main thing, of course, is taste. Food prepared in a clay pot acquires that delicacy, that refined quality and nobility of spirit characteristic of the highest achievements of ancient Russian cuisine.

Let's take, for example, a 3-pound piece of beef. We'll chop 2 large onions very finely and scatter them on the bottom of the pot. Then we lay the meat on top in one large piece, add peppercorns and a bay leaf, and put the pot into the oven on medium. Under no circumstances add water or salt. The pot will do all the work itself, and after 2 ½ to 3 hours you will have a tender meat dish, swimming in a mixture of onion and meat juices. In the meantime, you can prepare your sauce.

Fry some flour on a dry frying pan until it begins to smell of nuts (and it will, don't worry), then add 2 cups of sour cream to the flour. When it comes together, add 3 tablespoons of Dijon (if you don't have any Russian) mustard. Now you need to season the sauce with ginger and marjoram, add some garlic, and pour the sauce onto the meat. Then lightly season the dish. Another 1/2 hour in a warm oven, and you will have Merchant's Roast, the pride of the restaurant Slavic Bazaar.[2]

The meat will be so tender, well-spiced, and aromatic that it will simply fall off the bone. Add buckwheat kasha as a side dish, and you can invite your boss to a dinner *à la russe*.

You can prepare chicken or rabbit in the clay pot in the same way. And you can also cook a fish fillet in it; pour over top a mixture of milk and eggs, sprinkle generously with dill (1/2 cup) and in a half an hour serve the fish—tender as a young bride.

Cooking in the clay pot is very simple, because after you add the ingredients you don't have to do anything else.

The only problem is buying the pot. It's easiest to find one in stores that stock goods for people from Africa and the Caribbean Islands. In those underdeveloped countries, clay pots are normal and indispensable. One more thing—never put your clay pot on an open flame. It doesn't like that and will crack.

---

[1] These words are usually credited to F. M. Dostoevsky, but as S. A. Reiser demonstrated in an article in *Voprosy literatury* [Questions of Literature] (no. 2, 1968), they actually belong to Eugène-Melchior de Vogüé (1848–1910), who published an article about Dostoevsky in 1885 in *Revue des deux mondes* [Review of the two worlds]. De Vogüé's book, *Contemporary Russian Writers: Tolstoy, Turgenev, Dostoevsky*, was later translated into Russian and published in Moscow in 1887.

---

[2] The hotel and restaurant *Slavic Bazaar* opened in Moscow in the 1870s and became popular with local merchants as well as visitors to the capital. (Chekhov's Anna Sergeevna, in the story "Lady with a Little Dog," stayed here when visiting her lover in Moscow. Another of his characters, from the story "Peasants," was a waiter at the restaurant.) The historically real chef Vladimir Ivanov trained in Paris but maintained a menu in the "Russian style."

CHAPTER 2

Tea Is Not Vodka— You Can't Drink Too Much[1]

---

[1] This chapter title, like many in the book, is a common Russian saying.

It's safe to say that the national drink of Russia is vodka. To argue about this is foolish, and we'd rather not bother, but for the sake of the truth it is necessary. This is because there is also tea. Tea was brought to Russia from China in 1638, which was over a century before it was introduced in, say, England. Since then tea has become the symbol and sometimes even the center of Russian cuisine. The samovar has evolved into an icon of Russian life. Without tea you cannot understand the plays of Ostrovsky or Chekhov. Tea drinking accompanies key aspects of everyday Russian culture: long conversations about the meaning of life, the dacha, nightingales…[2]

Despite all of this, in Russia currently no one knows how to drink tea properly. As is often the case, one must go into exile to enjoy Russian cuisine. It's not that they understand tea here, but America has everything a true gourmet needs.

First of all, forget about teabags. Do not confuse ease of preparation or price with quality. You can make a cup of fabulous tea in just 10 minutes, and even the best drink does not cost more than three cents a glass.[3] Tea bags are packed with mere flecks of tea (that is to say, the waste).[4] What's more, the glue in the paper wrapper dissolves in boiling water, spoiling the whole flavor.

Another historical mistake is the practice of diluting the brew with boiling water. This custom originated with the poor and has grown into a superstition according to which strong tea is bad for your health. There is not one medical authority who would deny that strongly brewed tea is exceptionally valuable for good health. Many claim that Anglo-Saxons' predilection for this drink is precisely what allowed them to create their global empire. And the invention of the tea bag led to the demise of that empire.

Brewing tea is surprisingly simple. The only thing needed here is precision. Generally speaking, cooking is unlike any other art: diligence is more important than talent.

Heat up a porcelain teapot, scoop in some tea—1 spoon of tea leaves for every cup plus a spoonful for the teapot—pour in freshly boiled (not reboiled!) water. Let it steep for 4 minutes (if you leave it longer, it will turn bitter). Then stir and pour into a cup.

You can drink real tea with sugar, but don't use lemon or jam, which take away the smell. If you love English tea, observe the proper order: pour the tea into the milk, not the other way around.

It's hard to believe that a large part of humanity is unable to observe these simple rules and drinks swill when they could be enjoying an enchanting beverage.[5]

In any American city, there is a store where they sell the best sorts of loose-leaf teas. And there are tin cans packed with the famous English brand Twinings everywhere. The Indian tea Darjeeling is considered the best kind. All the high-quality black Chinese teas, such as

[2] Everyday life is related to the important Russian concept of *byt*. As semiotician and cultural critic Yuri Lotman has defined it, "*Byt* is the usual passage of life in its real and practical forms; *byt* is the things that surround us, our habits and everyday behavior. *Byt* surrounds us like air, and, like air, we notice it only when we don't have enough of it or when it is spoiled. We notice the specificities of the *byt* of other [cultures], but our own *byt* is elusive. We tend to consider it as 'life itself,' the natural norm of practical being. Thus *byt* is always in the sphere of practice, it is the world of things above all." From "Introduction: *Byt* and Culture," in Iu. M. Lotman, *Besedy o russkoi kul'ture: Byt i traditsii russkogo dvorianstva (XVIII–nachalo XIX veka)* [*Conversations on Russian Culture: Russian Noble Traditions and Lifestyle in the Eighteenth and Early Nineteenth Centuries*; this work has not been translated into English]. Dachas are obviously a significant part of Russian *byt*—they seem normal to the Russian and exotic to the foreigner. But nightingales are another matter—the nightingale is a symbol of inspiration and the presence of love in Russian poetry, as it is in classical and English poetry as well. But as V&G emphasize, the Russian dacha wouldn't be the same without the twittering of real nightingales. They are also a part of *byt*.

[3] Many American grandchildren of émigrés from the Russian empire grow up wondering why their grandmother or grandfather always talked about a "glass" of tea. Russians drink in cups or glasses, but the glass is a classic way to drink tea *à la russe*, particularly in a metal glass holder.

[4] The Russian word *brak*, translated here as "waste," means any second quality or defective merchandise that cannot be sold but must be disposed of somehow.

[5] Notice how V&G frequently prefer the short, even one-sentence paragraph. Throughout the text we have maintained their stylistic specificities as much as possible.

Yunnan, are lovely and aromatic. Ceylon is best for a cup of milky tea. And after a heavy lunch, nothing beats a Japanese green tea. The unusual Chinese tea Lapsang yields a gentle, smoky flavor. When added to any black tea, it summons nostalgic visions of tea parties in the woods.

For lovers of the exotic, the nomadic Kalmyk variation can be adapted for city conditions. Brew very strong, black tea in boiling milk (not water!). Add a pinch of salt and some butter.

Kalmyk tea will cure your hangover, a result that can only enhance overall health. Especially if you remember the ancient Russian proverb: tea is not vodka, you can't drink too much.

5

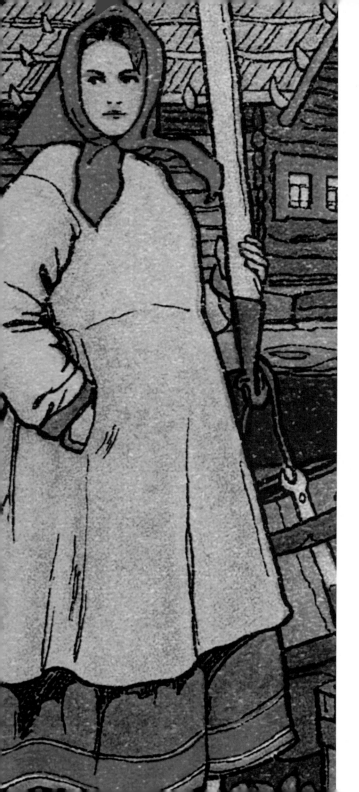

CHAPTER 3

The Scent of Cabbage Soup

What is the symbol of the Russian table? Vodka? Gefilte fish? Fighting?

Of course not. There is only one dish without which Russian cuisine is as unthinkable as an émigré newspaper without the old men of the Kremlin.[1] What is it? Cabbage soup, *shchi*.[2] Our entire culture and history are concentrated in this soup. And that's why we talk about *shchi* using not the singular, but the plural, not "it" but "them."[3]

Over the course of the first thousand years of Russian history shchi was the main and often the only dish on the Russian peasant's table. Then both shchi and the peasantry went into decline. Gradually this meal descended to the level of a pauper's thin broth, and it proceeded to seriously compromise Russian cuisine. If it smells like shchi in the house it must mean that the people living here are uncultured and backward. But at one time the scent of cabbage soup signified a special Russian hominess and coziness. "Here's the Russian spirit! Here it smells of shchi!" as the great poet wrote.[4]

Of course, in order to enjoy shchi, you don't actually have to put on a Russian peasant blouse and bast shoes.[5] You just have to prepare the shchi properly. Which may not be simple, but it's at least entertaining. Put the marrow bone and a good chunk of beef into the pot (don't ever use pork—that is a Ukrainian influence which is forbidden to us both as Russians and as Jews).[6]

Pour water over the meat and boil until it is partially cooked. Squeeze out some sauerkraut, put it into a clay pot, pour boiling water over it, and add 2 spoonfuls of butter. Cover the pot and place it in a warm oven; keep it there until the cabbage is soft. This will give the shchi the taste of having been stewed, something which you can otherwise only achieve by cooking it in a Russian stove. Since in America even the president doesn't have a Russian stove, this cabbage operation is unavoidable.[7] In another pot boil 2 or 3 dried mushrooms with a chopped potato.

Now you need to unite all the ingredients (the cabbage, the mushrooms and potato, and the liquid in which they were cooked) and add to the shchi finely chopped onion, carrot, turnip, parsley root and greens, celery root and greens, a few black peppercorns (crushed), 2 or 3 bay leaves, a teaspoon of marjoram, and some salt, and let it cook for about 20 minutes. Then take it off the flame, add garlic and dill, and place the soup pot into a warm oven for half an hour.

Before serving the shchi at table, it's good to add some pickled mushrooms cut into large chunks (we can't imagine where you will get them) and don't forget to add a dollop of a mixture of sour cream and cream to the soup plate when you serve it. Aesthetes sometimes include finely diced ham along with the root vegetables, but that is the devil at play.

[1] The expression "Kremlin Elders" (or "old men") refers generally to the politicians of the Brezhnev era and later, all of whom lived on well into their seventies. There was a sense in the USSR that young (men) didn't have a chance at power. And certainly Russian émigré newspapers followed the speeches and actions of those in power closely; after all, the Communist leaders were much of the reason that people emigrated from the USSR in the first place.

[2] *Shchi* is one of the classic Russian soups, and it also consists of only two letters in Russian, ЩИ. Generally speaking it symbolizes the simplest of Russian meals. As Pushkin wrote in the final chapter of his novel *Eugene Onegin*: "My ideal is now a housewife, All I desire is peace and quiet, A pot of cabbage soup, a proud toddler". A favorite Russian aphorism about the simple things in life goes: *Shchi* and porridge are our daily bread.

[3] Russian, like many languages, has a familiar and a formal "you." Since the formal corresponds to the plural, it may sometimes seem as though a really important person is addressed as if plural, or spoken about as "them" rather than him or her.

[4] Pushkin didn't say this. In the prologue to his first narrative poem, *Ruslan and Liudmila*, he did write: "There's the Russian spirit, there it smells of Rus'" (1820). V&G have rewritten this to emphasize the smell of cabbage soup.

[5] Bast shoes were made of woven fibers and worn primarily by peasants in Russia.

[6] Note that the authors do not always eschew pork products—just when it's convenient for their rhetoric.

[7] The Russian stove traditionally takes up 20–25% of the interior of a peasant home. Built of bricks, it has elaborate piping inside to turn the entire edifice into a source of heat as well as a place to cook food. Frequently the upper portion of the stove is turned into a berth which creates a warm bed for the young, infirm, or elderly, and sometimes it has benches for sleeping built in along the sides as well.

You must eat the shchi with an enormous quantity of fresh black bread, cut into slices a hand's breadth thick. On shchi day, no main dish is necessary. May God help you manage this soup course. The biggest problem is the consistency of the shchi. It must be very thick, so thick that a spoon can stand in the soup. But this recommendation, like all others of its kind—for example, "salt to taste, boil until ready"—is not particularly helpful for the cook. On the other hand, a reasonable person must have an inborn intuition and a sense of measure. People who don't shouldn't make shchi at all.[8] They will manage with less: for culinary purposes—a hamburger, for art—television, for sports—the card game of *durak*.[9]

---

[8] Notice how few exact measurements we find in this recipe. V&G would certainly argue that intuition (rather than precise measure) should guide the cook's hand.

---

[9] *Durak* (or "fool") is similar to slapjack or Egyptian ratscrew, all easy card games which are often the first game a child will learn.

C H A P T E R 4

Walking on Eggshells[1]

---

[1] The Russian original of the title is "The Value of a Hollowed-out Egg"—an idiom that means more or less "nothing." V&G would have loved the marketing slogan of the American Egg Board (1976): "The Incredible Edible Egg."

We have a complicated relationship with the edible egg. On the one hand, it's tasty and supposedly nutritious. On the other, if your child gets a rash, you may be reminded of the dirty word "diathesis," which is awfully close to the even worse word "diet."[2] Civilization has not invented anything more demeaning to human dignity than dieting. At least abstinence makes a certain sense—for example: economic sense. A heavy drinker spends far more money than a teetotaler. Not just on vodka, but also on related pleasures—taxis, decorative flowers, stupid presents like lamps or budgerigar parrots. Even sexual abstinence makes some sense (at least theoretically). They say that it increases creative potential exponentially. And it frees up more time for self-improvement and for cooking.

But there's not even a kernel of sense in dieting. First of all, health professionals don't have a clear understanding of which foods will be harmful or helpful for whom and under what circumstances. We know from our own experience that heartburn comes from tea, eggplant, milk, oysters, and so forth. But sometimes those foods don't lead to heartburn at all. The whole point is that the process of food absorption is not subject to the purview of universities. It is governed by higher spheres.

There is confusion about the egg's role in specific diets. Entire systems have been developed around eating hard-boiled eggs. Rumor has it that French ballerinas subsist on eight eggs a day, plus well water. Yet almost all other set diets, including Orthodox Christian fasting rules, exclude eggs entirely. The anti-egg movement is supported by Slavophile ideology and based on data from the Russian fairytale about Kashchei's death, which is hidden away in an egg. Since the Russian Kashchei is traditionally slender and gracile, his death must signify the victory of Western self-indulgence and its resulting corpulence.[3]

Actually, the egg is one of the most universal foods known to mankind and, significantly, one of the few that you don't get sick of if you eat them frequently. Apart from that, the egg is quickly and easily prepared, which has made it a fundamental part of breakfast, when time tends to be short. Eggs are fantastic raw, cooked (soft-boiled, coddled, hard-boiled), sunny side up (Russian-style), and scrambled (Ukrainian-style). But the pinnacle of egg culture remains the omelet!

In the old days, when master chefs were hiring, they would give the candidate one and only one test: making an omelet. This dish, laconic and demure, is simultaneously modest and clever—like a sonnet. On a thoroughly heated skillet you melt butter, and then pour in the egg-milk-flour mixture, already beaten to foaminess. (Only a little flour—1 teaspoon per 2 eggs. Together with the milk, you could add diluted sour cream and regular cream.)

As soon as the mixture thickens, immediately move the skillet to a preheated oven, where the omelet will swell and rise. The omelet should be eaten within seconds of being removed from the skillet.

[2] Diathesis, not a common word in English, describes a constitutional tendency or predisposition to a disease. This must have been a fancy way of saying what American pediatricians tend to say when they see a rash: "It may be contact dermatitis." In other words, we don't know why your child has developed a rash. The anxiety this induced in Soviet mothers was matched only by their anxiety about questions of diet.

[3] Orthodox dieting rules are extremely complex, in part because they were designed for people dwelling in monasteries rather than for lay people. In brief, there are four major "fasts" per year and many minor fasts, including most Wednesdays and Fridays, ranging in severity from no animal products at all to dairy-only days. Well over two hundred days of the calendar are "fasting" days of one kind or another. It is interesting that V&G add Kashchei the Deathless into their discussion of Orthodoxy and Slavophilism. Kashchei is one of the primary characters in the Russian folk tradition. Motifs from this tale were used in Nikolai Rimsky-Korsakov's 1902 one-act opera *Kashchei the Deathless* and in Igor Stravinsky's *The Firebird* (1910), which merged two traditional Russian tales. The most important thing for this chapter, of course, is that Kashchei's death was hidden in an egg.

The secret here is the uninterrupted process. The removal needs to be done quickly and the temperature should be just right. Only then will you be able to enjoy this dish. All kinds of side dishes are possible: an omelet goes with practically all vegetables, meat and sausage products, with cheese, fruit (including pineapple), and jam. The side dishes should be prepared in advance and already hot. You can then place them atop the omelet before moving it to the oven.

It is skill and constant refinement of technique that ensure the uninterrupted process. The most complicated thing is getting people to the table at the precise moment. It usually doesn't work out that way. You call your family. Your family answers: "Be right there!", but they don't go anywhere. They are busy with their own pointless tasks. You are sending them to hell under your breath, and they don't go there either. Now your small culinary triumph brings you no joy, and you feel like killing all the members of your family. A fantasy may develop from the proximity of knives and the oven, but that's a different kettle of eggs altogether.

11

КУРИНОЕ
ФИЛЕ

Back to the Chicken!

If you consider the avian realm from the viewpoint of an émigré cook, the chicken is the most enigmatic bird of all.

First off, it seems that everything we read in world literature was false. More specifically, we were misled by the plebeian ignorance of starving translators. It turns out that all their "I'll have a piece of *tsyplenok*" and "Make me a sandwich with *tsyplenok*" was really no more than ordinary chicken. That is, the heroine in question merely ordered "a piece of chicken," while the hero (who seemed back then to be so refined) turns out to be eating a banal chicken sandwich. Just like those translators, we were taught in school that chicken is *tsyplenok*, and *kuritsa* is hen.[1]

Secondly, we all grew up believing that chicken is more expensive, classier, and more prestigious than meat. If in a good production year for cattle, beef sold for 1.90 rubles a kilogram, then chicken would go up to 2.50. At one point, they sold broiler chickens for 1.60, but people were leery of them. The broiler fulfilled the zoological idea of developmental acceleration: the average chicken was the height of a seven-year-old boy and had an indeterminate flavor. The radically blue color of the broiler chickens scared off the pickiest eaters, and only employees of medical institutions could buy them without shuddering.[2]

When we arrived in Italy, it immediately became clear that we'd been kept in ignorance for many years. Chicken turned out to be cheaper than potatoes, bus tickets, and postage stamps. Émigrés went for chicken in a big way, and by the time we arrived in America we had a firm distaste for the bird, which even here is three times cheaper than *tvorog*.[3]

In the long years since, many took a different path: Back to the Chicken. The chicken's rehabilitation occurred on a totally new level, following the half-forgotten laws of the dialectic.[4] We can accept that it is neither a delicacy nor a disposable commodity. So now we say with confidence that chicken is the easiest start to a delicious meal. Especially if you have a mind to economize but no time to waste.

[1] The Russian word *tsyplenok* means "chick" in modern usage. Its antiquated meaning as the food product causes confusion for translators as well as a tinge of exoticism for Russian readers who had never been served anything but *kuritsa*.

[2] About medical institutions: I remember a friend of mine making rabbit stew when he had the flu one winter. His buddy told me: "Dima has easy access to rabbit, since he works in a lab." As a vegetarian, I was grateful to be able to beg off without offending my host [AKB].

[3] *Tvorog* was a hugely popular milk product in the Soviet Union, but it does not correspond exactly to anything we have in the U.S. Sometimes translated as "farmer's cheese" or "pot cheese," *tvorog* is a cross between ricotta, cottage cheese, and cheese curds, perhaps most similar to quark.

[4] Dialectical materialism was developed by Engels, Lenin, and Stalin and became the official Soviet interpretation of Marxism, a kind of state philosophy that represented the only acceptable method of studying history and society in the Soviet Union.

Use large chunks of chicken with roughly chopped onion: 2 medium-sized onions per pound of chicken. Put a small dab of butter in the bottom of the pot. Add bay leaf, peppercorn, chicken, and onion, but not an ounce of water! Add salt and leave to cook over a low flame.

Set about cleaning, making love, or engaging in self-improvement. In the kitchen, everything will proceed without your help. After about an hour and a half, you'll have a wonderful, succulent entrée, one which goes well with any side dish: boiled potatoes, rice, or pasta.

Chicken in onion sauce is particularly good because you can make it frequently by varying the ingredients. For example, add 2 or 3 dried mushrooms to the pot right from the start. A different variant: 5 minutes before removing it from the stove, add 1/2 cup of sour cream, 3 or 4 minced garlic cloves, a handful of chopped parsley or cilantro, a teaspoon of dried basil, marjoram or caraway leaves, or 1/2 cup of wine. Any of these ingredients will create a new dish since the onion sauce actively absorbs all seasonings and spices.

к варке

Суповая спаржа

The Soul of Solyanka

If you were to ask an acquaintance "What is *solyanka*?" he would start to describe the meaty stew served in restaurants. Considering that the general decline of culture has spread even to émigrés, it is only rare representatives of the first wave who remember that there can also be fish and mushroom solyankas.[1] These are really the most delicious.

But almost no one manages to make even the more famous meat solyanka properly. The first golden rule is to spare no expense on the ingredients. Although you can make a delicious *ukha*[2] from small, leftover fish and a fine borscht from cheap meat, a solyanka is only as good as the quality of its constituent parts: boiled meat, ham, frankfurters, boiled tongue, sausages (never under any circumstance smoked or partially smoked).

Slice some salted (but not pickled) cucumbers and toss them in the pan with onion, tomato paste and herbs (parsley, dill, pepper, bay leaf). Add this mixture to your bouillon. After about 5 to 7 minutes, add your chopped meats. After another three minutes add olives (only pitted ones) and capers. Quickly remove the soup from the burner. Before serving, spritz with lemon juice. Serve with slices of lemon and sour cream.

But a solyanka will never bring joy if you forget that the main thing in any soup is the broth. The bouillon should be spicy and robust. This is the second rule that is often neglected, even by those in communion with the first.

The solyanka first appeared in Russia in the seventeenth century, when the number of fasting days in a year fluctuated between 192 and 216. You can imagine that the fish and mushroom varieties were made more often than meat solyanka.

For a fish solyanka, the essential ingredient is sturgeon. Without sturgeon, however delicious it may be, it is nothing more than fish soup.

Boil down a small fish with the proper soup spices and the "waste" of the sturgeon: cartilage, head, scales. Strain this bouillon and add the same vegetables and spices as for the meat solyanka. After about 5 to 7 minutes, throw the pieces of sturgeon fillet in—they will cook up in about 7 minutes, too. To bring a little nobility to your solyanka, you can cook your fillet along with a bit of salted salmon: Siberian, humpback, or lox.

For a mushroom solyanka, you need dried white mushrooms. In the States you can find Italian and Polish varieties. For 2 liters of liquid, 6 to 8 mushrooms is enough. In a pinch, you can make do with dried champignons, but you'll need more of them. Boil the mushrooms, cut them into strips, and boil them again with sliced carrots, parsley root, and celery. Take 1 pound of sauerkraut and 1 1/2 pounds of fresh cabbage and braise them with onion and tomato paste, covered, until the cabbage is soft. Add the finely chopped and salted (not pickled) mushrooms. Simmer together for about 15 minutes. Before removing the solyanka from the flame, add black olives, capers and lemon juice.

Alas, there are some masters of mushroom pickling in the émigré community, but almost no one makes salted mushrooms. Even so, you can at least make a mediocre mushroom solyanka. Even without salted mushrooms it's worth making this soup with its distinctive taste and aroma.

After all, the main value of Russian cuisine is its soups. It's no surprise that spoons appeared in *Rus'* some four hundred years before forks did.[3]

[1] Although many Jews emigrated to the United States from the Russian empire starting in the 1880s, traditionally emigration from Russia in the twentieth century is divided into three "waves": those aristocrats and others fleeing the Bolsheviks after 1917, the displaced persons and other immigrants who arrived after World War II, and the "third wave" of émigrés in the 1970s and 1980s, primarily Jews permitted to leave for Israel (many of whom chose the United States, Canada, or Australia once they arrived in Europe), or intellectuals such as Solzhenitsyn and Joseph Brodsky who were ejected from the Soviet Union by the Brezhnev government.

[2] For more on ukha, see chapter 20.

[3] *Rus'* is the historical name of the lands inhabited by Eastern Slavs.

MONTS OURALS.

VÉRITABLE EX

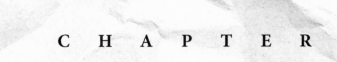

CHAPTER 7

Fish Tales

Countries can be classified as maritime, mountainous, or forested. Russia is a country of rivers. The abundant, navigable rivers of the East European plains were the cradle of our homeland. Since Russians have always been too lazy to build roads—from the times of Rurik until the present day—rivers have always been important routes of communication, linking the Vyatichi, the Krivichi, and even the white-eyed Chudes into one great realm reaching from Cuba to Afghanistan.[1]

This environment brought forth one very important culinary development—fishing.

Freshwater fish have always occupied pride of place in Russian gastronomic tradition. Oysters, beluga, sturgeon, and even minnows were more plentiful in Russia than anywhere in the world. And no one knew better than the Russians how to prepare them.

But all of this is in the past. Today's Russians, excluding the village prose writers, of course, believe that processed meat is better than any fish.[2] Although even proper sausage has been lost along with our national roots.

In America, fish usually resembles pieces of cotton breaded and deep-fried to such a degree that the burnt crust causes heartburn and a steadfast dislike of all foods that aren't hamburgers. What is to be done?[3] America has also forgotten its roots. After all, in *Moby Dick* Herman Melville mentions a restaurant that served two hundred kinds of boiled fish.

Melville generally knew what's what. It's not for nothing that in his novel they eat their fish boiled. Fish is a delicate substance that cannot be fried in bread crumbs.[4] It needs a gentle touch.

[1] The Vyatichi and the Krivichi are two medieval Slavic tribes, ancestors of the Russians and Belorussians. The Chudes referred to a Finnic tribe, one of the founders of Rus′ and are frequently spoken of in folk legends as "white-eyed." But Cuba? Afghanistan?

[2] Village prose writers include Valentin Rasputin, Viktor Astafiev, and Vasily Shukshin, among others. Generally from Siberia themselves, they wrote stories chronicling life in the countryside and villages of Russia, places where language, mores, and relationships were under assault by contemporary social changes.

[3] The phrase "what is to be done" regularly appears in Russian speech and may or may not always be meant to evoke its most famous uses: by Nikolai Chernyshevsky in his 1863 novel, *What Is to Be Done?* and then again by Vladimir Lenin in a political pamphlet of the same name (published 1902).

[4] V&G here use the lofty sounding term "substantsiia," which is fairly unusual in this context.

Let's assume that you don't want to mess with bones, so you buy fresh fillets. Now comes the cooking. Keep your wits about you. First, create an appropriate environment for the fish. The fish needs it as much as you do. Make some broth using parsley roots (and greens), onions, carrots, celery, dill stems, and one potato. And of course bay leaf, allspice, pepper, and salt.

Boil some pickle brine separately and add it to the broth. It will give the fish density and preserve its white flesh. Now cut the fish into large chunks and add it to the broth. And here we have the trickiest part: you mustn't boil the fish too long. It will be ready in 5 to 7 minutes. Serve it "free." Just mix a little melted butter with lemon juice and pour over it. This will already be really something. However, if you don't want to rest on your laurels, you can go on and make the fish into something else … something on a whole new dizzying level.

Pour a glass of white wine into a deep frying pan with a tight lid. Add thinly chopped onion, celery greens, fennel, and parsley. And again, bay leaf, pepper, and salt. Add tarragon and some saffron infusion. Squeeze some lemon onto the fillet pieces. Once the liquid comes to a boil, carefully arrange the pieces of your fillet in the pan, making sure enough liquid remains to cover the fish. Now, reduce the heat, and whatever you do, keep the fish from coming to a boil again. Cover the pan tightly and after 10 to 12 minutes, serve. Maybe, to someone with crass tastes, this dish will seem too delicate. What is to be done, if people now prefer strength and endurance to weakness and tenderness, even in women? But don't give up! Well cooked fish is a culinary masterpiece. Furthermore, it's a tribute to our Slavic ancestors.

CHAPTER 8

Vital Forces

And to drink? No, no, we're not going to talk about vodka. We want to discuss so-called nonalcoholic drinks. In the Soviet Union there was no debate—everyone drank lemon-flavored soda pop because there wasn't any other kind of soda pop.[1] Once here, everyone rushed to try all the American varieties, especially Coca-Cola. Gradually people calmed down. They got bored, and they also figured out that all sodas contain harmful ingredients: caffeine, cocaine, carcinogens, sodium chloride, potassium cyanide.[2] Almost every Russian émigré has gone through the iced tea stage—we fancied this drink could be a noble compromise, a symbol of how we could combine abiding tradition with progressive flexibility.[3] But we live in a country that's mad about vitamins, and sooner or later everyone comes around to fruit and vegetable juice.

And that's how it should be, because neither man nor nature has conceived of anything tastier. We are talking about freshly squeezed juices of course. Despite our confidence in the American Food and Drug Administration, canned juices are just the pathetic bastard brothers of delicious, nutritious natural juices.

Which is why everyone should buy a juicer. Then the creative process can really begin.

The fact is that when making juice, you can and must mix fruits and vegetables. This matter is just as personal as choosing a bride, but in both cases some basic rules apply.

We generally divide juices into three categories: morning, before-dinner, and dessert.

The point of morning juice is to raise your vitals and help the transition from sleep to wakefulness. Therefore tart juices are preferred, particularly citrus. You can't go wrong with half a grapefruit and 2 oranges. For more pep, you can add 2 slices of lemon or lime.

A before-dinner drink should stimulate the appetite in those who lack it; for everyone else juice is simply a delicious liquid *zakuska*.[4] A mixture of vegetables is good. Start with a base of tomato juice and add from there as you see fit: celery, parsley, dill, cilantro, peppers.[5] The usual proportion is 1 tablespoon of greens for every 2 tomatoes. This combination can be recommended to Bloody Mary lovers.

Dessert juices are milder, sweeter, and thicker. Apples pair well with carrots (1 carrot for every 2 apples), strawberries (2 or 3 berries per 2 apples), and pears (1 per 2–3 apples); 2 or 3 sweet tangerines are delicious with a piece of pineapple, a small banana, a peach, or an apricot.

But the most important part of making juice is the joy of experimentation. After all, there aren't many areas of creativity in our lives that are enjoyable, are good for you, and don't consume a lot of time and money.

19

[1] The general embargo on Western goods made soda a rarity in the Soviet Union. Apart from the Soviet soda *Baikal*, Pepsi was the only product of its kind, officially sanctioned starting in 1973. The most common carbonated beverages came from vending machines. *Gazirovannaia voda* ("water with gas") could be purchased with or without citrus flavoring syrup.

[2] A reference to Coca-Cola's supposed/early inclusion of cocaine as an ingredient. Here V&G are surely joking about chemistry. Potassium cyanide was the drug in suicide capsules for spies and whatnot.

[3] Cold drinks (with the exception of vodka) are an abomination to Russians, for whom an iced beverage is an invitation to illness. Children with a history of ailments are often refused all things cold for the sake of their health. For this reason the opening scene of Mikhail Bulgakov's *Master and Margarita* (in which Berlioz and Bezdomny ask for cold beer on a hot summer day, but eventually settle for warm apricot juice) seems more satirical to a Western audience than it did to Russians, for whom it was practically realism, both for the temperature of the beverage and for the likelihood of advertised goods not being in stock [TF].

[4] An appetizer in its original definition, of course, "stimulates the appetite." For Russians the *zakuska* table is a matter of pride, an important part of hospitality, and a place where Russian cuisine really shines.

[5] In fact, Anastas Mikoyan introduced juice-drinking to the Soviet Union after his trip to the United States in 1936. He deliberately chose tomato juice instead of orange juice, favored in America, as the most feasible for mass production in his own country.

CHAPTER 9

An Unfashionable Virtue

The grim old cliché "no accounting for taste" was invented by people who lack taste themselves. Truly there's no arguing with bad taste. It must simply be conquered. Especially when it comes to cuisine.

Because in the case of cuisine, there are plenty of simpletons who believe that food is some kind of personal, deeply intimate activity. But unlike the other modern arts, gastronomy does not bend to the will of the individual. It has strict laws, rules and regulations. Let the avant-garde have their war on traditional values. A decent person should be somewhat conservative. At least at the table.

Educated and cultured people never eat caviar without butter. Nor do they spoil it with raw onion, as even the best American restaurants do. Their innate (or acquired) sense of harmony will not allow them wash down herring with *kompot* or eat soft-boiled eggs cold.[1]

The culture of food says more about a person than erudition and the ability to use a handkerchief. A chef, even an amateur one, simply has no right to be a lackey with no solid moral principles. Moral relativism ("let them eat as they please") is incompatible with cooking. Good cooking requires law and order.[2] And cooks don't need to let their imaginations run wild—they just need to observe the fundamentals. For example, you cannot prepare a good soup without carefully skimming the foam from the broth and wiping the sides of the pot with a paper towel. If you don't cut out the eyes of a potato, the dish will taste and smell of damp earth. If you use the same knife to cut fish and meat, the latter will be ruined completely. If you brew tea with re-boiled water, it will turn bitter.

Even those who boast of loving escargot and bouillabaisse tend to forget these basic steps. But negligence takes its own revenge (and not only in the kitchen).

Now cooking is becoming the most widespread hobby in the world (and particularly among men). Perhaps because today there are so few solid foundations in any field of intellectual activity.

These days, discipline doesn't fit our lifestyle. It's an unfashionable virtue. Still, the noble and ancient culinary arts are impossible without discipline. They instill in us a respect for the little things, for order, even for systematic living. (After all, couples who dine together every day are the last to divorce, or so they say.)

Good cooking is a war between order and the amorphous nature of life. When you stand at the stove with a spoon in your hand (a wooden one, of course!), be warmed by the thought that you are a soldier in the struggle with world anarchy. The kitchen, in that sense, is the front line.

---

[1] *Kompot* is a stewed fruit drink.

---

[2] The original for "good cooking" here is *khoroshaia kukhnia*—and of course *kukhnia* means a variety of things: cuisine, kitchen, cooking. Throughout the book the authors play with its multiple meanings.

CHAPTER 10

I'll Have the
Kharcho!

Our people have embraced internationalism in one sphere only: cuisine. We treat our foreign friends to *pelmeni*. Russian restaurants lure customers to Brighton Beach with pilaf. American cookbooks include the walnut sauce *satsivi* under "Russian Foods." The Soviet pavilion at the World's Fair served borscht and shashlik. This is clearly a catalogue of the achievements of Northern, Central Asian, Ukrainian, and Caucasian cuisines—but a great integration occurred, and now it is all known as Russian cuisine. Even so, we must never forget that the Caucasian branch constitutes the clearest, sharpest, most lively, and fanciest aspect of our cuisine. And of the Caucasian cuisines, Georgian shines brightest.

Ask any true Muscovite gourmet, and he will burst into tears at the word "Aragvi."[1] Those who have actually travelled through Georgia (as opposed to just visiting the resorts) forever cherish the memory of the simple, inimitable aroma of Georgian dishes, each of which inspires its own poem, as Pushkin rightly said.[2]

It is a deep, even criminal, delusion to consider Caucasian food to be merely spicy. While the preparation does usually include red pepper and often garlic, it would take a truly uninspired individual to just throw a handful of pepper into a subtle dish and think that will give it a Georgian flavor.

Georgian cuisine is not just spicy, it's flavorful! And in its spice bouquet, pepper and garlic occupy one of the lowest places, surpassed by cilantro, parsley, tarragon, basil, cinnamon, clove, saffron, *khmeli-suneli*…[3] It's the fresh spices that make the difference. That is to say, using herbs rather than dried spices adds a subtle flavor and contributes a spicy, invigorating effect.

Try to make *kharcho*—that same kharcho served in any ordinary cafeteria. But do it right, and you will see that this is like no soup you've ever tried.

First of all, kharcho is not made with lamb, but with beef. Generally speaking, Georgians prefer beef to all other forms of meat (its only rival is chicken). So, take 2 pounds of lean beef. Cut the meat into 1-inch cubes, pour 3 liters of water on top and cook for about an hour and a half. Take the meat out, strain the liquid through a colander, bring it to a boil, and sprinkle 1/2 cup of rice evenly over the surface. Add salt and put the meat back in. After about 10 minutes, it's time for the first set of spices.

For the first set: finely chop 4 medium-sized onions and fry them with 1 tablespoon of flour, one parsley root, a bay leaf, and a dozen crushed peppercorns.[4] After 5 minutes, pour in half a cup of freshly-crushed walnuts.

The second set of spices is added after 5 more minutes and consists of 2 tablespoons of [chopped] parsley greens, 1 teaspoon of dried basil, and 1/2 teaspoon each of red

[1] The Aragvi was a famous Georgian restaurant in Moscow founded in the 1930s—according to legend by Soviet government and Communist party functionary Lavrenty Beria, the same who in 1941 became head of the KGB. The restaurant was frequented by the Soviet political elite.

[2] An apocryphal attribution—but then, Pushkin gets credit for many things in Russian culture.

[3] *Khmeli-suneli* is a Georgian mix of dried herbs, including basil, spicy red pepper, cilantro, dill, celery leaf, bay leaf, mint, marjoram, parsley, savory, and other herbs.

[4] It's fun to realize that in Russian stores, and Russian recipes, things come in tens rather than in dozens. So you might hear a Russian housewife say "pick up a ten of eggs on the way home from work." Here the recipe calls for "a ten of crushed peppercorns"—but really, will the outcome be worsened in translation to a dozen?

pepper and cinnamon. Only then add the acid. Georgians use *tklapi* (dried *tkemali* plums).[5] But we don't have *tklapi*, so you should pour in 1/2 a cup of pomegranate juice, or, in a pinch, 1/2 a cup of tomato paste.[6] For the classical variant, you need khmeli-suneli, but we don't have that either. Russian stores usually have *adjika*, but if you decide to use that, skip the red pepper.[7]

In 5 minutes, turn off the flame. Add 5 cloves of crushed garlic, 2 tablespoons of cilantro greens, and 1/2 tablespoon of basil or celery leaves, and let it stand for about 5 minutes.[8]

This soup you've made bears almost no resemblance to what you're used to calling kharcho, and you will finally realize the state of ignorance you've been living in all these years.

[5] Here the "acid" could be lemon juice, lime juice, vinegar, but V&G prefer the Georgian sour fruit if available.

[6] Probably don't use 1/2 a cup of tomato paste if you're making this recipe! [AKB&TF]

[7] *Adjika* is a hot red pepper sauce, sold commercially or at Georgian markets.

[8] Again, here we see evidence of chefs who know what they are doing and don't necessarily clue in the amateur. You will want to chop the greens finely if you're making this soup.

такана риса. Посолить и положить мясо обратно. Минут через 10 ввести первую порцию пряностей.

В первой порции: обжаренный с одной ложкой луки мелко нарезанный лук — 4 средних луковицы; 1 корень петрушки; лавровый лист; 10 раздавленных горошин перца.

Через 5 минут после этого всыпьте 0,5 стакана свежетолченных грецких орехов.

Через 5 минут и состоит из 2 ст. ложек зелени петрушки, 1 ч. ложки сушеного базилика, 0,5 ч. ложки красного перца, 0,5 ч. ложки корицы. Тогда е вводится кислая среда. Грузины используют клапи — сушеные сливы ткемали. Но у нас тклапи ет, поэтому надо влить в суп 0,5 стакана анатового сока, в крайнем случае — 0,5 стакана оматной пасты. По классике надо добавить мели-сунели, но у нас и этого нет, зато в русских агазинах бывает аджика — добавьте ее, ключив в этом случае красный перец.

Через 5 минут выключите огонь, добавьте 5 зубчиков толченого чеснока, 2 ст. ложки зелени кинзы, 0,5 ст. ложки зелени базилика или сельдерея, и дайте настояться минут пять.

То, что получилось, почти ничем не напоминает тот суп, который вы называли харчо, и вы осознаете, наконец, в каком невежестве жили все эти годы.

хмели-сунели

СОСТАВ: кориандр, с... петрушка, базилик ого... шафран, цветки барха... пажитник голубой, чабер садовый, соль

CHAPTER 11

Sharlotka, a Russian Name

Everyone loves sweets, though far from everyone will admit it. Grown men and vodka-drinking women are particularly ashamed of this sin.

A sin is a sin. It's easier to succumb to it than to fight it. However, things are not so simple with desserts in America. A society that has declared war on calories significantly limits opportunities for pastry chefs. It's possible to believe that censorship is a boon to literature, but in culinary matters prohibitions are perilous.

This is why the sumptuous, elegant pastries in the windows of bakeries often turn out to be merely bland, ephemeral decorations. Something like paper flowers. And what is a first-class chef to do if vicious public opinion forbids him to use butter, sugar, or even batter? He creates an elaborate stage set.

People need an alternative, and we want to offer the émigré reader one such option. It won't work for Americans, because this alternative is sweet, rich, and very delicious. It's called a *sharlotka*.

The word comes from the French name Charlotte, to which the Russian language added a suffix, one that can be perceived as either affectionate or pejorative. Vladimir Dahl understood the sharlotka to be a round cake with jam.[1] But this is not the case.

In fact, a sharlotka has nothing to do with the French or with jam. It's an ancient Jewish treat, and here's how you make it.

Take a stale loaf of white bread and remove the crust, then cut it into thick slices and soak them well in a mixture of eggs and cream.[2] While the bread is soaking, core and skin some apples and cut into thin pieces. Sprinkle with powdered sugar and let rest until the sugar dissolves. Grease the walls and bottom of a clay pot (we will assume you have one) with butter. Start with a layer of bread and sprinkle it well with powdered sugar, cinnamon, and crushed nutmeg. Then a layer of apples, and so on, continuing to the very top of the pot.

Generously add pats of butter, inserting them into any crevices. Sprinkle granulated sugar over the top to give it a pretty brown color.[3] Cover and place it in an oven preheated to medium. In about 40 minutes, if the apples have softened, you can serve the sharlotka. It's best to eat it immediately, while it is hot.

By the way, for our laziest readers we can suggest a simplified recipe invented by German students, a dessert known as a "Poor Knight."

Soak some pieces of bread in cream, sprinkle with powdered sugar, and brown in butter in a frying pan, like toast. Nothing simpler.

Of course, no one gets skinny eating sharlotka. And they say that eating a lot of bread is harmful. On the other hand, life is generally a harmful thing—after all, it always leads to death. But once you've eaten a piece of sharlotka, that inevitable destination seems somehow less frightening.

[1] Vladimir Ivanovich Dal' (or Dahl) (1801–72) was a Russian lexicographer. His greatest work is the four-volume *Explanatory Dictionary of the Living Great Russian Language* (published 1863–66).

[2] The Russian here is *baton*, which is an elongated loaf somewhat less skinny than a baguette—not a sandwich loaf, as implied in English by the term "white bread."

[3] Here V&G use *kolër*, not originally a Russian word.

CHAPTER 12

The Anti-Semitic Lily

In Russian literature, without a doubt the most anti-Semitic plant is garlic. The quills of the great Russian authors expended restless decades on the stems and bulbs of this harmless garden herb. If the classic writers had been more learned, they might have known that garlic is related to the lily, and perhaps the pastoral beauty of its lineage would have given them pause. But in their ignorance Pushkin, Gogol, Kuprin, and virtually all of the others considered it their duty to label garlic as the most unpleasant attribute of Judaism.

However, throughout human history there have been peoples who have revered garlic just as much. The Persians used it in everything. The Romans loved it. The Arabs couldn't get enough of it. In our day, garlic cuisine is fashionable with such enlightened nations as France and Spain. One prominent chef of old even somehow calculated: "Peace and prosperity visit those places where garlic has found a place on the menu."[1] We won't try to test this daring hypothesis and will only note in passing that the Russian classics were wrong. Garlic is used far beyond the borders of the Pale of Settlement.[2]

It's just that Jews have always been more health-conscious than the other peoples of Russia, and in their eyes garlic is a panacea. In various times and places it has been used to treat heart and kidney problems, dog bites and toothaches, asthma and hangovers, rheumatism and hair loss. (In all times and places there has been a belief that garlic aids libido, but that's really a topic for the book *Russian Sex in Exile*).[3]

Thus it seems Russian Jews have done well to eat garlic. Whatever mistakes they made in going about it are a different matter.

[1] Xavier Marcel Boulestin, "It is not really an exaggeration to say that peace and happiness begin, geographically, where garlic is used in cooking." Boulestin (1878–1943) was a French chef and restaurateur who moved to London, wrote cookbooks for English-speakers, and became the first television cook on *Cook's Night Out* for the BBC. His opinion of garlic has been widely quoted.

[2] The Pale of Settlement was the section of the Russian empire between 1791 and 1917 in which Jews were permitted to live. Its boundaries varied, but generally speaking it corresponded to present-day Lithuania, Belarus, Ukraine, Moldova, Poland, plus parts of eastern Latvia and western Russia.

[3] It's amusing to contemplate a whole set of books—Vail and Genis's *Russian Cuisine in Exile* sharing a bookshelf with Gleb Struve's *Russian Literature in Exile*. Who would write *Russian Sex in Exile*? Perhaps the anti-Semitic one-time émigré and well-known sex tourist Eduard Limonov?

In the preparation of almost any dish there is a period of 2 to 3 minutes when you can add the garlic. That is, the moment you turn the heat off, plus or minus 1–1.5 minutes. If you add the garlic earlier, it will either disappear without a trace or, if there's a lot of it, lend an unpleasant bitterness to the dish. If you add garlic to a dish that has already cooled, it will overpower the other ingredients, and there will be no other taste at all. Those who so offended the dainty nostrils of the Russian nobility preferred this second method of adding garlic.

There are still a few more general rules for the correct usage of garlic, which it behooves any respectable person to know. Garlic strikes an inharmonious chord with fish, but enhances any seafood: prawns, scallops, crab, lobster.[4] Of all meats, garlic is best paired with mutton. "Sweet" southern garlic (this variety is big, almost like an onion) is right for salads, pairing well with tomatoes, cucumber, and watercress.[5]

An aioli sauce complements boiled meat, lobster, crab, and boiled and baked vegetables. For a proper aioli, mix 2 tablespoons of crushed garlic with 1 egg yolk, 1 tablespoon of Dijon mustard, 1 tablespoon of lemon juice, and 1 cup of olive oil. Add salt and pepper and whip the mixture until it thickens.

It is even simpler to make a hot escargot sauce. Heat 1/2 cup of olive oil with 2 tablespoons of chopped parsley and 1 teaspoon of dried tarragon, add 1 tablespoon of crushed garlic and, after a minute, turn off the heat. The sauce is unrivaled with prawns, scallops, or boiled or steamed broccoli.

The whole trick is that really, for culinary purposes, only freshly crushed garlic will do. Not the powder and not that stuff in the jar, chopped by dubious people at some undisclosed time. The work may be tedious, but it's brief and rewarding. Garlic, when properly prepared and added at the right moment, makes for a perfect lily.

[4] In the Russian, Vail and Genis here show a predilection for "émigré-speak"—instead of the Russian plural word (*moreprodukty*) they use the English singular "seafood," then placing it in the dative case.

[5] V&G may have in mind here what we know as elephant garlic.

CHAPTER 13

A Chameleon Lunch

Only the most naive believe that the heart of the American people belongs to baseball. In fact, it should be obvious to everyone that the national sport in the USA is barbeque. On a nice Sunday, the smoke of innumerable grills clouds the sky, as in the Indian days of old. American cuisine worships the steak, and the grill is its prophet.

The art of grilling steaks consists of the ability to buy the right piece of meat. All the rest is as simple as multiplying by ten: light the charcoal, put the steaks on the grill, turn them over, eat. The less the chefs get involved in the preparation of the steaks, the better off they are (the steaks, that is). The simplicity (not to say primitivism) of this culinary choice fits the national character. We once read the following instructions on the box of a tube of toothpaste: "1. Unscrew top. 2. Squeeze paste onto toothbrush. 3. Screw top back on tube." The theory of classical barbeque comes close to these instructions.

Well, you can't argue with steak. It is filling, healthy, and even tasty. But it's pretty boring. And an excursion to the countryside implies collective merriment around a convivial table. Who would bother with grilling in gloomy solitude? From our point of view, the ideal barbeque should consist of representatives from every species in the animal and plant kingdoms, especially since they can all be cooked on one surface. And there's no need for pots and pans. A roll of aluminum foil will do fine.

Start with a fish steak. The best choice is a swordfish—the expensive delicacy also featured in *The Old Man and the Sea*.[1] Marinate the fillet overnight in pomegranate juice and then grill it in foil for about 25 minutes.

The grill enhances even the most everyday foods. For example, ham, which we usually associate with the same old open-faced sandwiches.[2] Brown both sides of a thick slice of ham, douse generously with lemon juice, and serve with a decorative slice of canned pineapple.

As far as vegetables go: wrap them carefully in foil and roast. Just don't yield to childhood memories and try to make potatoes in a foil jacket. It takes a potato two days to achieve the requisite consistency on a grill. A sweet pepper bakes much more quickly and turns out better. Cut off the stem, remove the seeds, and put a small piece of butter inside. In half an hour, you will find a magnificent garnish for a meat dish on your grill. And if the foil doesn't burst, the pepper will retain its moisture.

Cooking on a grill is great, and the food is always a success. You work up a real appetite in the fresh air, which is the constant component of outdoor meals. Hunger nullifies any blunders by the cook. To calm yourself you can pretend that you really only went on the excursion for the sake of the fresh air. And like a chameleon, you can exist on air alone.[3]

[1] Hemingway's influence in Soviet Russia, from the 1930s through the 1980s, cannot be overestimated. For Russian writers he and his characters represented a kind of personal freedom that would have particularly interested those who planned to emigrate, or who ended up doing so, like V&G. The best book on Hemingway in Russia is still Raisa Orlova's *Hemingway in Russia: A Half-Century Long Affair*, published in Russian (Ann Arbor, MI: Ardis, 1985).

[2] The Russian word for this, *buterbrod*, hints at its German roots.

[3] Pliny the Elder, in *The Natural Histories*, writes, "[The Chameleon] is the only animal which receives nourishment neither by meat nor drink, nor anything else, but from the air alone." While it's true that chameleons leave their mouths open for long periods of time and are fairly abstemious in their diets, they actually eat insects.

With chicken things are not so simple. This bird prefers to be eaten fully cooked, and roasting over coals implies a certain amount of residual blood. That's why it's good to marinate the drumsticks the day before you head into the wild in a standard shashlik marinade: that is, cover the chicken with a layer of onion, pepper, and salt, and pour a cup of dry white wine over it. Properly marinated chicken cooks in about 20 minutes.

Kidneys on the spit can add a piquant overtone to an outdoor meal. Wash the kidneys carefully, skewer them, and roast over the coals, turning frequently. Veal or lamb is best, and you mustn't forget to serve the kidneys with lemon.

In Search of Appetite Lost[1]

---

[1] Here V&G are evoking Marcel Proust and his *À la recherche du temps perdu* (1913).

Some people assume that a good meal requires good food. Or a fork and spoon. Or money. Or companions. But this is incorrect.

You can get by without these things. There's only one thing a good meal can't do without: an appetite. Even the most sophisticated gourmets sometimes fail to keep this irrefutable fact in mind. Hunger enhances enjoyment in the same way that aesthetic desire or lust heightens joy in a museum or in bed. We must guard our hunger with the same reverence as we do our love for women and for art.

But let us leave our daring analogies and turn to harsh reality. Do we only eat when we are hungry? Nothing of the sort! Even in this most intimate of matters, our affairs are subject to external circumstances. It is not the belly, but the alarm clock that summons us to breakfast. Not nature, but the boss determines lunch time. Even our feasts are shadowed by the burden of absurd traditions. Really, who can enjoy New Year's dinner at three in the morning?[1]

All this leads to a devaluation of culinary sensations. In losing the freedom to eat when we want to, we lose interest in food altogether. And here the idea of "nutrition" rears its ugly head: those loathsome vitamins, proteins, and cholesterols. A man forgets about his immortal soul and starts to regard himself as a cow, which requires high-calorie feed to achieve … what? maximum health?

In order to unlearn this bad habit, you must reformulate the very concept of food. Of course, we eat to live. But, to adjust this worn aphorism slightly, we might say, "To live well, you must eat well."

A sensible man doesn't bow to mainstream standards. He doesn't throw himself at a vulgar *buterbrod* at the first sign of a free moment, simply because the moment is free. He won't groggily stuff himself with those indistinct wood shavings known by the foreign name of "cereals" just because everyone else does.

Oh, no, he will treat his appetite like first love, tenderly and romantically. He will nurture his appetite with imagination and sunset walks. He will devote the best hours of his day to it, and not just add it to the blur of his other affairs. He will wait for the moment when hunger illuminates the shades and nuances of his food. He won't sit down at the table until his appetite transforms the meal into a feast.

No, better not to eat at all than to eat listlessly and without appetite. Of all the sensual joys, only this one does not devolve into vice. It is accessible to us from the cradle to the grave.[2]

Of course, there are many ways to prod appetite along its unhurried path to a healthy hunger. Some propose an aperitif (Starka, pepper vodka, or Pernod).[3] Others favor enticing hors d'oeuvres (Vorschmack, oysters, anchovies). A third group (the most foolish) talks about diet.

In our view, the truth lies deeper. Real appetite is born of a creative enthusiasm for food. If you peruse the menu before you, carefully consider each ingredient, do not begrudge the time devoted to arranging the meal, consult with your aesthetic sense, heed the wisdom of culinary authorities (Molokhovets, Gogol, Gilyarovsky), and sit at the dining table as poets sit at their writing desks, then and only then will you be able to appreciate the meaning and measure of the truest of all human passions: the affinity for food.[4]

They say that physical labor also helps. We don't know about that, we've never tried.[5]

[1] New Year's celebrations were particularly important during the Soviet era, when religious holidays were frowned upon. Joseph Stalin reinstated the official New Year's holiday in 1935, and traditional Christmas trappings (decorated pine trees indoors, gift exchanges, "Father Frost" and his helper *Snegurochka* [the Snow Maiden]) were added to champagne toasts at midnight. A full dinner often followed.

[2] This expression combines two common sayings. In classic nineteenth-century literature we read in Ostrovsky's 1860 play *The Storm*: "I am married, and I will have to live with my husband to the very grave." And from Maxim Gorky's 1898 story "The Scoundrel": "From the very cradle I have been unable to tolerate moralizing."

[3] Various vodkas: rye, pepper, and anise-seed based, respectively.

[4] Elena Molokhovets (1831–1918) was the author of the popular cookbook *A Gift for Young Housewives*, first published in 1861. Nikolai Gogol (1809–52) is well known for the descriptions of Russian and Ukrainian food and foodways in his 1842 novel *Dead Souls* as well as in his short stories and plays. Vladimir Gilyarovsky (1855–1935) wrote *Moscow and Muscovites* (1926), a portrait of the Russian capital in pre-Soviet days. Anecdotes, descriptions, and lively voices have made this work of journalistic prose a favorite among Russians, and it is an excellent resource to help understand the role food played in Moscow life.

[5] Lev Tolstoy was famed for lauding the simple life: vegetarianism, abstinence from alcohol, tobacco, and sex, and manual labor. The hilarity of this laconic final paragraph comes in its juxtaposition with the previous long-winded detail-filled sentence about how one should approach food.

МЯТА ПЕРЕЧНАЯ

CHAPTER 15

Our Underwater Life

Of all of the edible novelties available in the West, the strangest for us is the array of foods that fall under the universal term "seafood." It is probably best that we too use this alien word, since there is no match in Russian (except maybe the phrase "gifts of the sea").[1] If memory serves, this was the name of the best restaurant in Murmansk, one of two major attractions in the city, the other being the first sobering-up station for women in the country.[2] Regardless, émigrés were tickled by the taste and varieties of "seafood." Except for those who keep kosher, of course. Alas, Judaism throws up obstacles to any aquatic creatures that don't have scales. We don't want to sink to the primitive level of atheistic propaganda, but really, to willingly deprive oneself of smoked eel …[3]

Émigrés quickly grew accustomed to seafood, the more so since mollusks and crabs are just like us. Judge for yourself: like mussels, we always try to nestle up to something stable; like shrimp, we try to blend into the surrounding environment; like oysters, many of us lack teeth; like crabs, we have an ample bosom and a small head; like lobsters, an extended torso. The same that is said of scallops can be said of us (like calamari, we are cephalopods in our own right): our young hitch themselves to anything, while adults freely lounge on the bottom.

Now that we have felt our kinship with sea life, come to know and love the creatures, we can commence eating them.

With crabs, lobsters, and shrimp, it's best just to boil them. It's not worth yielding to decadent temptations to bake, fry, or grill them. Crustaceans (and crabs, by the way, are simply short-tailed versions of the crawfish so beloved of all Russian beer drinkers) are most delicious when boiled in a strong bouillon of roots and spices. Throw a lot of celery, parsley, and parsnip, a bay leaf and some peppercorns into the water. Salt well and boil for about 10 minutes. You need to boil the crustaceans separately: 3 minutes for shrimp, 5–6 for crabs, and 8–10 for big lobsters.

It is the sauce that adds variety and subtlety to the dish. The classic choice for crab and lobster is melted butter with garlic and lemon juice. For shrimp, it's best to thicken this sauce with a spoonful of starch or flour dissolved in cold water, and add dried parsley, tarragon, or basil. A mixture of ketchup and horseradish gives a distinct and sharp flavor. Gently heat this mixture with sour cream and throw in your boiled shrimp.

Any sauce that's good for shrimp is also good for scallops. The zoologist knows them as the muscle of the bay scallop, but to the chef they are simply one of the finest seafoods. Don't boil them in advance: 2 or 3 minutes in a boiling sauce is enough. Overcooked scallops taste like rubber.

Shrimp and scallops go very well with poached or boiled fish, or with grilled veal. These crustaceans flavor the main dish with a festive touch. Remember that tarragon is the best seasoning for this type of seafood.

You shouldn't cook oysters at all, since it's not feasible to smoke them at home, and that's the only manner of preparation worthy of the oyster. But everyone knows you can eat them raw with lemon, and there's nothing better with champagne or white wine. It's no mistake that billions of oysters are harvested in France every year.

Mussels are the cheapest of the mollusks, and they work well in one very delicious main dish. Get a frying pan hot with oil, finely minced garlic, and parsley greens, and then throw in the mussels still in the shell. The heat will open the shells, and the mussels will bring forth their juice. Then empty the contents of the pan into a pot of boiled spaghetti and mix it all up for a few minutes over a medium flame.

---

[1] See above, note 4 to chapter 12.

---

[2] Starting in 1940 the Soviet era drunk tank, or sobering-up station, came under the Ministry of Internal Affairs rather than the Health Ministry. Seriously intoxicated and comatose citizens were taken to the hospital, but the ambulatory or "medium-intoxicated" ended up in the *vytrezvitel'*. Drinking in public was less socially acceptable for women, but there were such cases.

---

[3] Eel is not kosher, since you can't scale it without tearing the flesh.

Белый гриб (боровик)

Масленок

Груздь

Mushroom Metaphysics

Mushrooms—like some of our acquaintances—occupy a middle-ground between plants and animals. Scholars still haven't decided if they have a soul. But anyone who has found a *borovik* in the forest has no doubts. White mushrooms are robust and assertive, *lisichiks* are coquettish and fussy, *smorchoks* have a wizened soul, while *rizhiks* are all Slavophiles (surely Vladimir Soloukhin was a rizhik in his past life). Only champignons have no souls, since after all they are cultivated, not wild.[1]

In Russia, before the Revolution, each person consumed fifty kilograms of mushrooms yearly. Now in Moscow markets one mushroom costs one ruble.[2] And in this we see evidence of our country's spiritual impoverishment.

For émigrés maintaining ties to the fatherland can be difficult, but it is possible. One easy method is to buy dried boroviks imported from Poland or Italy. And the most traditional way to serve this expensive food is in mushroom soup.

Soak about 5 mushrooms in cold water (no need for exact proportions; we're not Germans, after all). In about 2 hours, retrieve the mushrooms, cut them up, and fry them. Don't dump out the soaking liquid. Save it to add to the soup if guests should arrive. Add carrots, onions, and parsley stems to the broth. After an hour, the mushrooms will be cooked and will fill the kitchen with a fantastic aroma. Now come the dilemmas. One culinary school of thought says to add fried onions to the soup, while another suggests fishing out the mushrooms, frying them with more onion, and throwing them back in. Then you have to decide which you prefer, vermicelli or pearl barley. It doesn't matter whether you put in potatoes or not, but you absolutely must add dollops of sour cream and sprinkle with chopped dill. Whichever variant you choose, the result will knock your socks off.

Mushroom meatballs call for patience, if not art. Boil dried white mushrooms, mince them finely, and add sour cream, melted butter, eggs, pepper, minced onion, and breadcrumbs. Then roll the mixture into balls, roll the balls in more bread crumbs, and brown in butter. You can add these meatballs to a mushroom bouillon, or serve them separately, with sour cream.

But, in general, dried mushrooms are not meant to be made into specialized dishes. The idea is to throw them in wherever whimsy and prudence dictate. Your only limits are parsimony and palate. Like gold, dried mushrooms add dignity to any mixture and can never ruin a dish. For example, fry a finely minced onion over a very low flame. When its juices begin to flow, throw in precisely one pulverized mushroom cap. In half an hour, add sour cream, and pour this sauce on whatever you like: cutlets, boiled tongue, roasted meat, potatoes. Every dish will acquire a noble color and aroma.

[1] A *borovik* is a cep or porcino mushroom (*boletus edulis*). A *lisichik* is a chanterelle (*Cantharellus cibarius*), while a *smorchok* is a morel (*Morchella esculenta*) and a *rizhik* is a saffron milk-cap (Lactarius deliciosus). Vladimir Soloukhin (1924–97), born the son of a repressed peasant, was a poet and author who became an advocate for the beauty of the Russian countryside and a defender of Russian Orthodox Christianity, in particular indicting the Soviet government for destroying monasteries, churches, and icons. In 1967 he published a popular book about mushroom gathering entitled *The Third Hunt*. The champignon is the common or button mushroom, also sometimes known as crimini mushrooms (*Agaricus bisporus*), not to be confused with the prized white mushroom.

[2] Household incomes in the late Soviet period varied, but the majority of households earned between 100 and 200 rubles a month. See Michael V. Alexeev, "Income distribution in the USSR in the 1980s," *National Council for Soviet and East European Research* (Washington, DC, 1992).

Ancient Russian cuisine recommends adding dried mushrooms to any soup: vegetable soup, shchi, even ukha.[3] Mushrooms were eaten with kasha, poultry, fowl; they were an indispensable component of cooking. This advice is sensible, albeit pricey. Mushrooms can provide their own flavor to a dish, or enhance a foreign flavor with typical Russian largesse.

In America, unfortunately, a mushroom always means a champignon. The misfortune is in the word "always," since champignons themselves are not guilty of anything.[4] They can be pungent and demure, like the French culture that produced them. (Although the French themselves prefer our boroviks, or truffles, a mushroom as rare as chastity.)

With champignons, the best approach is to cut them up and toss them into a dry frying pan. In about ten minutes, when all of the juices have seeped out of them (for this part leave them uncovered), add a browned onion and some sour cream. Now boil the mushrooms, covered, for five minutes and serve. Remember that guests were treated to this very dish at the Palace of Congresses, where champignons were considered a sign of détente.[5]

There is also the anti-culinary approach to champignon eating, which consists of eating them raw. For this, you must take only the freshest, whitest specimens and cut them lengthwise into thin strips. Every piece should remind you of a flat image of the three-dimensional champignon. Then toss the mushrooms with watercress and drench them in sour cream diluted with lemon juice. Of course, this is no mushroom solyanka, but it does have a certain chic.[6]

Gluttony, an intrinsic aspect of our world-view, prevents us from writing about mushroom hunting. Suffice it to say that in this pastime, as in no other, the gentle soul of the Russian becomes manifest.[7]

[3] On *shchi* (cabbage soup), see chapter 3. On ukha, see chapter 20.

[4] Note the personification, true of all the mushrooms in this chapter!

[5] The Palace of Congresses was built in 1961 at the initiative of Nikita Khrushchev in the Moscow Kremlin. It holds 6,000 people and was designed for meetings of the Communist Party of the Soviet Union. The Palace also serves as a concert venue.

[6] See chapter 6 on solyanka.

[7] Gentle, but jealously guarding secrets of the craft? How else might we explain the association with gluttony? In this, perhaps, the paradoxes of the Russian soul are revealed.

CHAPTER 17

The *Botvinya* Battle

Even in such an important realm of human activity as the preparation of cold soups, folly and chaos reign. Either you're served a bowl of brown water with coarsely diced onions and told it is "gramma's" *okroshka*, or you're offered a svekol'nik prepared under the watchful eye of a senior rabbi and processed commercially.[1] Of course, you can always avoid going to visit your friends. But if that's the way you want it, you may as well not have emigrated.

One reason we cannot get along without cold soups is that we now live in the south. Even those who made it to Chicago still live on the same latitude as Tbilisi. New York aligns with Baku, San Francisco with Ashgabat, Los Angeles—good heavens!—with Serhetabat [both of the latter in Turkmenistan]. We used to call it "Kushka," the place "beyond which you couldn't be exiled"—because it was the southernmost point in the Soviet Union. It's really tough for those émigrés who can't even find a geographical analogue in our homeland for the place they now live. True, Houstonians and New Orleanians have hope: south of Kandahar battles are raging, and soon the thirtieth parallel will also be ours.[2]

It's strange that in a country as far south as the United States there are no native cold soups. The best you can do is a Spanish gazpacho or a Jewish/Belarusian svekol'nik. It falls to us to transform this uncivilized nation.

To bring bottled svekol'nik to a reasonable state, you must work with it. First, you must come to terms with the most important thing: it's not enough to just chop up some boiled meat, hard-boiled eggs, cucumbers, scallions, and dill. You will end up with some kind of liquid-y salad, and though soup is known to be liquid, the flavors have to come together. Take 2/3 of the foods listed above, cut them up finely, and run them through a meat grinder or a food processor fitted with a large attachment. Pour the beet liquid from the bottled svekol'nik over these ingredients and leave it to chill at least 2 hours. When the soup is already served at table, add the last 1/3 of the unprocessed fixings to the soup bowls. This way you will be preparing actual soup, not just a random collection of edible ingredients. And if you stir 1 teaspoon of dill weed into a mixture of 2 teaspoons mustard with 2 tablespoons each sour cream and lemon juice, you will achieve a svekol'nik worthy of guests. (It's even better, obviously, if you boil up the beets yourself: you can make extra and store the juice in the refrigerator indefinitely, using as needed.)

In the Middle East they prefer soups made with cultured milk products. The principles for preparing them are the same. Cut up 5 large cucumbers and mix with 2 minced garlic cloves, 1 cup of shelled walnuts (to make shelling the walnuts easier you will need to heat them in the oven, about 15 minutes at 350°), 1/2 cup of diced scallions, 2 tablespoons of minced dill, salt, and pepper. Run 2/3 of the ingredients through the meat grinder, cover with 1.5 liters of kefir, and set aside to cool. Before serving, add the

[1] Svekol'nik, cold beet soup, kosher of course, is easily obtained in any Jewish aisle of the grocery. *Okroshka*, another popular Russian cold soup, consists of vegetables and a hard-boiled egg and often meat, all served in a broth of *kvass*, which is the Russian fermented beverage made from bread.

[2] This tongue-in-cheek remark refers to the Soviet-Afghan war. The USSR invaded Afghanistan in December 1979. The war continued for nine years, with final troop withdrawals in February 1989.

last 1/3 of the solid ingredients and spritz with lemon juice. It's remarkably refreshing, so who cares if it's a favorite food among Arabs. The Arabs you dislike haven't got time to mess with soups, they simply eat raw meat.[3]

We brought with us abroad cold green shchi—delicious during a heat wave. Alas, it's hard to get sorrel here. They have it in Brighton Beach, but what don't they have in Brighton Beach? Recently someone there traded an Order of Lenin medal for a used air conditioner. The spinach you can get here is too neutral, but there is one other green émigrés have criminally neglected—watercress. In the Soviet Union men with peaked caps and gravelly voices sold this green, calling it *tsitsmaty* and asking a ruble a bunch for it.[4] Watercress—which has a sharp, bitter taste—makes excellent cold shchi, although you have to boil it fairly long, about 15 minutes.

By the way, you can make sorrel or watercress soup with a light fish bouillon instead of plain water. Just boil up some pieces of fillet and flavor with lemon juice. This soup is refreshing and filling.

A true masterpiece in the genre of cold soups is also made with fish: *botvinya*. Soak beet tops and sorrel until soft and then dice them finely with cucumber, scallion, and dill, pour *kvass* over to cover and add horseradish, mustard, and lemon juice. Boil pieces of smoked dried fish in a little water for 2 to 3 minutes. You can use sturgeon, salmon, or halibut. Add the fish to the broth and let it stand in a cool place for at least an hour.

Botvinya should transform life in Houston, if they can read Russian there. We wonder how things stand with botvinya in Kandahar?

[3] A message to fellow Russian Jewish émigrés in Israel? Or this may refer to the legendary (if apocryphal) diet of the Mongols—raw meat tenderized beneath the saddle.

[4] The image of a Georgian vegetable trader should rise up before the reader's eyes.

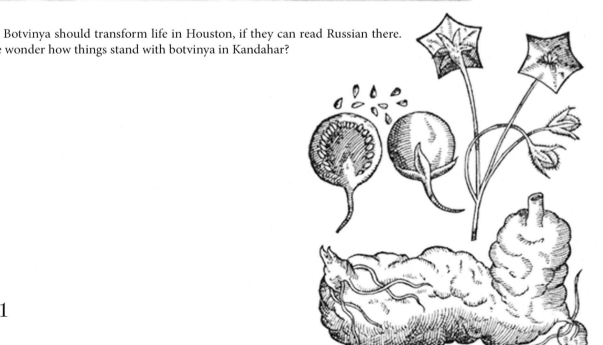

41

CHAPTER 18

Running with
the Sheep

In many cultures, mutton is an indispensable dish.

But not in ours.

Lamb doesn't suit Slavic traditions. That is to say, it is at odds with pickles, sauerkraut, and vodka. It congeals in our unaccustomed throats and sits in an undigested lump in our bellies until our next meal. All because we don't wash it down with hot green tea or cold red wine.

Russian cuisine makes two exceptions for lamb. The first of these is pilaf, which pairs well with poverty, because, as the tired cliché goes, pilaf is cheap and easy. And usually inedible.

The second exception is considerably better: shashlik, the delight of our picnics. And of course we make it the Russian way, not the Caucasian way.[1] That is to say, we marinate the meat in vinegar, onion, and pepper (mountain peoples prefer pomegranate juice and actually use beef). You can also fry up an onion in the leftover fat. This high-calorie slop really does the trick when you're hung over, and you can forget about your diet until Monday.

But you'd have to agree that the lamb dishes on our menu are criminally few. And it wouldn't take much to add to it, just patience and hard work. They say these virtues can help you achieve any goal. For example, putting toothpaste back in the tube.

The secret to making a good lamb dish is in how you cut the meat. Here you must be ruthless. Remove every bit of fat until the lamb shank is transformed into a bowl of perfectly red cubes. Michelangelo approached a block of marble in roughly the same way. And what was the result? Immortality.

If there's no skin, no fat, and no veins left on the meat, then there won't be that peculiar lamb aftertaste, which spoils the memory of any feast. The aftertaste will be gone, but the taste remains.

Well-cubed meat should be aesthetically pleasing: it should make you want to eat it raw. Incidentally, there's nothing wrong with that, but better to make something out of it. For example, you can make *Lula Kebab*.[2] Finely mince your meat and onion using a meat cleaver. Mix with cilantro and parsley, add salt and a good amount of pepper. Then wrap the mixture around skewers (or just make small, oblong patties) and roast on the grill. Anyone can make this, since no émigré lacks a grill, just like no one lacks relations.

[1] On Georgian and other Caucasian cuisines, see chapter 10 above.

[2] Traditional *shashlik* is a skewer kebab, while the ones described here are mince kebabs.

However, it won't do to get hung up on the primitive (albeit very tasty) Lula Kebab. Throw 1/2 kilo of very diligently dressed lamb into a meat grinder or food processor, add 1 egg, 3 tablespoons of oil, 1 whole onion, some flour, and a lot of pepper, and grind the meat until it achieves a certain airiness. Now we're talking quality. Roll the meat into little balls about the size of a walnut, bread them in egg and farina, and quickly fry them in oil.

Kololaki, as this Armenian dish is called, should always swim in sauce. And this is very easy to achieve. Pour 1 cup of broth into a pan (canned broth is fine). Cut up 2 onions, add 3 tablespoons of tomato paste, 1 tablespoon of flour, 1 tablespoon of oil, 1/2 teaspoon of wine vinegar, pepper, parsley, and basil. Simmer for about 10 minutes and pour over the lamb balls. You can leave the kololaki to cook in the sauce for about another 15 minutes. This recipe only takes a long time to read; it cooks up very quickly.

Now we've gotten what we wanted from the lamb: exoticism and tenderness. If we could just get the same from our wives...

CHAPTER 19

Hang Him from the Klyukovo Tree!

Yes, Russia is considered to be a backward, savage country. Yes, Russia is loathed and feared. But for the love of God, what does this have to do with Russian cuisine?

Mao Tsetung was no Jesus Christ either, but does the reputation of Chinese cuisine suffer due to the Cultural Revolution? Did the world turn its back on sausage and Bavarian beer because of the crimes of the Third Reich?

During our years in emigration, we have come to the conclusion that the West is catastrophically ignorant in matters of Russian food. What's more: this ignorance, like any ignorance, is obstinate and aggressive.

But better they know nothing at all of the existence of Russian dishes. Instead, the custom on this side of the Iron Curtain seems to be to pervert our national legacy in a monstrous fashion.

What could be worse than *Life* magazine's recommendation to eat Ukrainian borscht ice cold? Breaking through a crust of grease to slurp down a liquid that congeals on the lips? You don't need to dedicate your life to Sovietology to figure out that borscht is eaten steaming hot, with black bread, garlic, and sour cream. Borscht is not nuclear physics, it's not a secret, like Andrei Sakharov's phone number. To paraphrase Solzhenitsyn, everyone knows what borscht is, but no one understands it.[1]

Let them toss ice in their vodka. Let them sip it like aging coquettes. But how can we tolerate their habit of eating raw onion with delicate Beluga caviar? That's like hammering in nails with a microscope. To describe the innumerable Western transgressions against our cooking, you'd need to compile a whole volume. And one has been compiled. The reputable American publisher Simon and Schuster released *The International Pocket Food Guide* to explain the specificities of all the world's cuisines.

Unfortunately, it includes a Russian section. The charlatan who wrote the guide is named Quentin Crewe, and he lives in Cheshire, England. The publisher does not give a more detailed address, apparently fearing the vengeance of slandered peoples.

What the aforementioned scoundrel writes about Russian cooking is a symphony of ignorance, for which the very first phrase could serve as the overture: "Russian cuisine, in one sense, does not exist."

And this after all of Europe adopted the Russian appetizer table, the richest in the world. For Quentin Crewe, our aspics and jellies, our salted fish and caviar, along with all the various pickles which caused such a furor in Paris, simply don't exist. Naturally, he doesn't even know that Russian cooking has the greatest repertoire of soups in the world. Among these, shining like the diamonds in his British crown, are shchi, ukha and okroshka.[2]

But the best is yet to come. The book catalogues the gems of Russian cooking, "those dishes which appear most frequently" on restaurant menus. Here's what we found on the menu: "*Chornye olivi, klukovi sup, krevetki sup, malyoki sup, sup kholodetz, gribnoi sup, ugor v vino, gruzinski plof, indushka s kashtanami, chakapuli, vareniye kartoshki v smetane, spinat s orekhami, tyanushki.*" To the publisher's shame, the author gives the names of all these dishes in Russian.[3]

[1] Solzhenitsyn wrote "Everyone knows what Communism is, but no one understands it."

[2] On shchi, see chapter 3. For ukha, see chapter 20.

[3] The Russian, transliterations, and translations of Quentin Crewe's menu items all have errors of one kind and another. Even *vareniye kartoshki v smetane*, a bastardized version of boiled potatoes in sour cream, is translated as "baked potatoes with sour cream and scallions."

The Simon and Schuster International Pocket Food Guide

Menu Decoder

How to choose a restaurant

Find your way around the menu
How to order   Where to eat
Local specialties   What to choose
Personal favorites   Seasonal suggestions
What to drink with your food

All the world's major cuisines described in detail
Entries grouped as you find them on the menu
Glossaries of useful foreign words
Over 10,000 alphabetical entries
Culinary terms explained

An essential companion for the traveler
Traditional recommendations   Vocabularies to help you order
Gastronomic experiences   Maps of major food areas
Regional variations   Typical dishes

We are absolutely certain that the Soviet authorities—always quick to react—would immediately have the director of a restaurant with such a menu impaled. In this one concrete case, we are in absolute solidarity with the Soviet authorities.

In addition to cataloguing his meals, which resemble the lunch of a middling conceptual artist, the author (whom the preface calls an expert) gives explanations, too. For example, according to him *forshmak* is made with beef, herring, and potatoes mashed with cheese, and shashlik is meat with mushrooms.[4]

If we had our way, we would force the whole Simon and Schuster Publishing House to subsist on hot dogs made of beets and hamburgers with ice cream until the end of their days in retaliation for this book. Lex talionis: an eye for an eye, a tooth for a tooth.

Maybe it will seem to some that we shouldn't experience such strong feelings in response to such an insignificant matter. But what are feelings for, if not to wield in defense of this most sacred material?

[4] *Forshmak* is made with salted herring baked with potatoes, sour cream, and onion (not to be confused with forshmak made with meat, a German dish). Another variant (the "Odessa" version) is made with herring, egg, and apple, with butter. Shashlik is grilled cubes of meat or minced meat. For more on shashlik, see chapter 18.

CHAPTER 20

Ukha—Not Just Soup, but Pure Pleasure

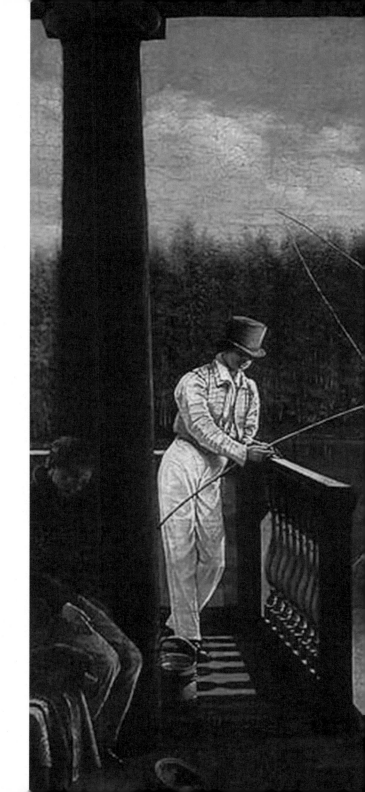

The mournful inventory of irredeemable losses suffered by émigrés is just as endless as the list of newly obtained advantages. As for aquatic fare, the main achievement—an exotic one—is the abundance of seafood. The main loss—real ukha.

If a foreigner tries to create ukha according to émigrés' recollections, he will discover to his surprise that its main component is vodka. The truth is, we recall the scenes that go along with ukha: the light rain, the gray twilight, the poorly pitched tent, the bonfire that continually goes out, the soot-covered pot, the bickering in hoarse whispers for fear of startling the fish. There is nothing better than this dreary picture, because everyone knows what comes next: wet bottles with their labels sliding off, and the divine taste of ukha made with freshly caught river fish.

Ukha and vodka are inseparable in the mind of a real Russian—like Pushkin and Lermontov, the Elephant and the Pug, black eyes and passionate eyes.[1]

And of course, ukha is a ritual. It may be a ritual above all else. But there is still the culinary point of view according to which ukha is a hot, watery fish soup. In Rus′ in the old days any rich soup (*pokhlyobka*) was called ukha—even a meat soup. In one of the best descriptions of a dinner in all of Russian literature—from A.K. Tolstoy's novel *The Silver Prince*—we read: "They brought various soups and three kinds of ukha: white chicken, black chicken, and saffron chicken."[2] But by the seventeenth century ukha referred to fish soup only.

It's important to disassociate ourselves—decisively—from any effort to present regular fish soup as ukha. Ukha must have a pure, clear bouillon, and thus cannot include a roux, grains of any kind, fried onions, or sautéed vegetables. Ukha is fish, spices, and herbs, and you can't add anything else except potato and carrot—and that's it.

The best ukha is made from a) small, b) fresh, c) river fish. Of these three main points, the hardest to achieve is point c. And here there's nothing to be done: the mournful inventory of irredeemable losses… (see beginning). For the broth you can use small ocean fish.

[1] These references run the gamut from classical nineteenth-century Romantic poetry to the famed gypsy song "Black Eyes, Passionate Eyes," which might very well be sung around a campfire that featured ukha and vodka. "The Elephant and the Pug" is a fable by Ivan Krylov about a little dog who barks at an exotic elephant being paraded through the streets.

[2] A.K. Tolstoy (1817–75) was a poet, dramatist, and historical novelist. He and Leo Tolstoy were second cousins. *The Silver Prince* is set in the sixteenth century. Its subtitle is "A Tale of the Terrible Times."

[3] The Russian language is filled with proverbs, and as is obvious in this book, they are frequently used in speech and writing.

[4] In Russian, soup is always served in a plate, but the term actually refers to a bowl with a wide rim, what in formal dining services is called a "soup plate" in English.

Boil the fish with a ratio of 2 pounds per 5-liter pot of water. Once the fish is soft, discard it ruthlessly. Strain off the fat and put the broth to simmer on a low flame, adding onion, parsley root, celery, coriander root, bay leaf, peppercorns, and salt.

In 20 to 30 minutes add the carrots—cut in thin strips—and the potato, tarragon, and basil (fresh or dried). After another 5 to 7 minutes add pieces of fish fillet. For this you need a noble fish: choose cod, trout, or whitefish. If you can find it, use sterlet. The fillet should cook several minutes.

The more varied your selection of spices and the more you add, the better the ukha. As the proverb goes: it might not be fishy, but it's ukh-y.[3] Still, don't skimp on the fish fillets; use about two pieces per plate of soup.[4]

Heat up several strands of saffron in a cup of hot broth and pour into the soup pot after the soup comes off the flame. The ukha will become golden and aromatic. Throw a piece of butter into the pot, let it stand three to four minutes, sprinkle with dill and green onion, and serve.

The question of whether to serve vodka—in a carafe so cold its surface weeps with condensation—with the ukha is a criminal one and as such does not deserve an answer.

CHAPTER 21

Our Native Tongue[1]

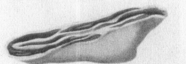

11. Ше...

12. Руль...

9. Пашинка

13. Заре...

10. Лопатка

14 и 15. Гол...

---

[1] Vail and Genis wrote a famous book called *Rodnaia rech'*, which is also translated *Native Tongue*. The "tongue" of this article is *yazyk*—meaning both the language and the physical tongue.

We have a friend who was expelled in his third year of Meat and Dairy School for systematic embezzlement. Thanks to his efforts, we are quite well-versed in food technology, particularly in the primary parts of a cow.

Everyone knows that a cow has a tenderloin. Some suspect that it has a soul, while others believe that they were a cow in another life, or will be one in future. How far this is from a state of true, deep knowledge! We could really shine in conversation with an expert: shin, groin, rear pastern, spindle… But alas, since we emigrated there's no one to have a chat with.[1]

It's on the shelves of the supermarket that the cow reveals its secrets. That's where we encounter a wealth of innards. In our homeland they were referred to by the foreign word "subproducts," which obscured them from view along with Finnish furniture and the works of the surrealists.[2] We had no idea that cows, like cameras, come complete with diaphragms. The similarities stop there: A Kodak only has one button, while cow diaphragms are those white, nylon-bedspread-looking things that you see Puerto Ricans buying by the dozen in the streets.[3] On top of that, who could have imagined that cows have little "books" inside of them?[4] Which means they have something that a lot of émigrés lack. The cow stomach is composed of tripe, rennet, and a "book." You may eat the first two parts, but not the third. (Of course not, that's the one you read!).[5]

But the most important part of the cow is its tongue. We encountered the tongue at home too. There was no tastier appetizer in a restaurant than jellied tongue (unless you're from Riga, in which case you prefer lamprey). The idiotic Dahl defines tongue as "a meaty projectile in the mouth," but then what do you expect from a foreigner![6] No one needs a tongue in their mouth; even having one at all can be dangerously unhealthy. And incredibly tedious. But on a platter? Now we're talking!

The simplest way to prepare tongue, of course, is to boil it and serve it garnished with greens, pickled cucumbers, and horseradish. But even here, skill and specialized knowledge come in handy. You should prepare the broth with as much care as you put into writing your last will and testament. An onion, two sticks of celery, two carrots, parsley root, bay leaf, allspice, black pepper, and salt—it's important not to forget anything, because the end result will be in direct proportion to our initial efforts. We want our tongue to be spicy and aromatic.

Jellied tongue is also a really delicious appetizer. The jelly plays an important role, so add white wine (half a cup per liter of broth) and a pinch of basil or marjoram to the stock. Bring it almost to a boil, but don't let it boil. Strain the liquid, then thicken with gelatin and pour it over chunks of tongue that have been laid out in a pan. Avoid any unnecessary decoration that might alter the delicate taste of the jelly, such as hardboiled eggs. Jellied tongue should only be accompanied by carrots, neatly sliced and boiled along with it.

[1] This recalls the eternal problem of emigration: the loss of language. Nabokov famously complained about this, writing in his memoir *Speak, Memory*: "My fear of losing or corrupting, through alien influence, the only thing I had salvaged from Russia—her language—became positively morbid" (265). V&G were writing for their own community and in that sense were able to savor their native tongue. Of course, in living in the United States, they were subjected to the same linguistic pressures as any immigrant writer—they just chose not to be histrionic about it.

[2] The implication here seems to be that the foreign name "subproducts" (the viscera of the animal) was off-putting for Soviet consumers: another form of censorship.

[3] A version of this chapter in another edition talks here about opera singers and their diaphragms.

[4] The folds of a cow's stomach.

[5] We are emphasizing the corniness of this joke by adding an exclamation point to V&G's comment. Although, as F. Scott Fitzgerald famously wrote, "An exclamation point is like laughing at your own joke."

[6] See note in chapter 11. Dahl was born to a Danish father and German mother in what is now Lugansk, Ukraine. His German-sounding surname reminds us that the Russian empire was multinational. The comment is particularly amusing in the context of this book written by émigrés in the United States for an émigré readership across the world—i.e., for an audience who had become foreigners.

If you fry large pieces of boiled tongue with onions, pour in two cups of broth and cover with a layer of sliced potatoes (about the same size as the pieces of tongue), you'll have a delicious main dish in 30 to 40 minutes. While the mixture simmers, you can add a combination of spices to create a festive, unforgettable dish—Tongue, Caucasian Style. For this you need 2 tablespoons of finely chopped parsley, 1 tablespoon of coriander, 3 cloves of chopped garlic, and 2 tablespoons of crushed walnuts. Just as cold tongue requires cold vodka, red wine completes this meal.

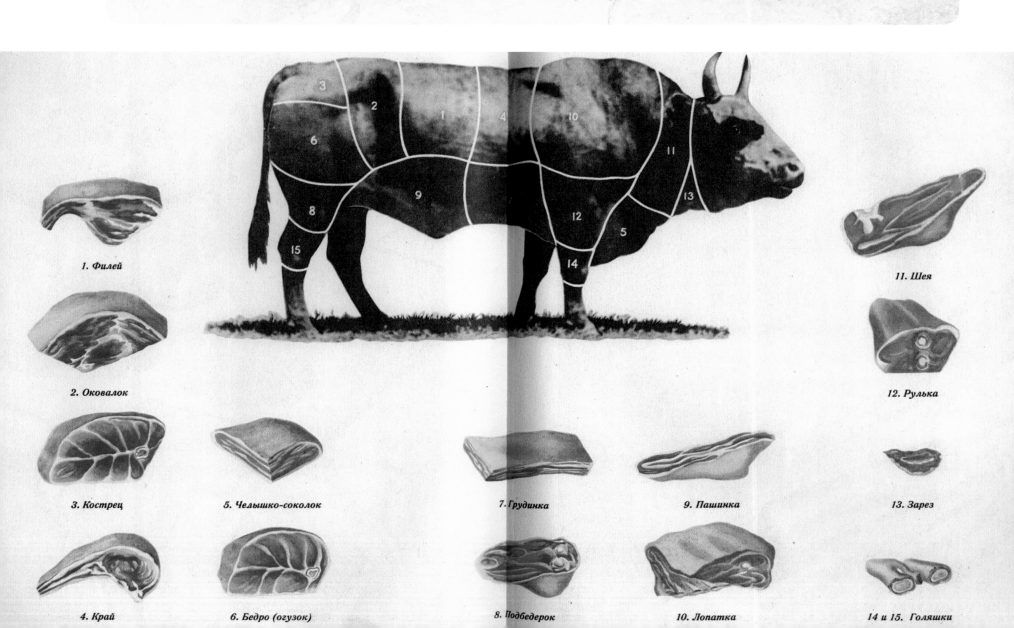

1. Филей

2. Оковалок

3. Кострец

5. Челышко-соколок

7. Грудинка

9. Пашинка

11. Шея

12. Рулька

13. Зарез

4. Край

6. Бедро (огузок)

8. Подбедерок

10. Лопатка

14 и 15. Голяшки

CHAPTER 22

Jewish Penicillin

Usually mixed marriages between Russians and Jews do not suffer from an increase of mutual hatred.[1] But there is one question which is sure to cause a spat. What soup should we make—borscht or broth?[2]

Both dishes are marked with national traits, and they are as different as a snub-nose is from a hooked one.

However, this opposition—like any national difference—is inappropriate in matters culinary. Being by nature compromisers, we recognize the merits of both kinds of soup. But it's easier to make broth. If borscht can be as capricious as Gogol's prose, then broth has a certain soberness and even some measure of Jewish mercantile prudence: when you make it, you get your first and second courses at once.

Nevertheless, the simplicity of broth is merely an illusion. It requires at least expertise, if not art.[3] It's not for nothing that non-Jewish Americans see some kind of mystery in elementary chicken soup and believe in its healing powers. That's why they nicknamed it Jewish penicillin.

Sadly, there's no real mystery. But there are two secrets.

First of all, you must always cook broth on a very low flame. Secondly, don't skimp on the root vegetables.

Take an ordinary chicken (by the way, a rooster is preferred, it will provide more fat) and cover it with cold water. When the water comes to a boil, you must very painstakingly skim the foam and even wipe down the sides of the pot with a paper napkin. The clarity of the future broth depends on this operation: a good broth should be clean and clear, like the water in the Red Sea near Eilat.[4]

Now lower the flame to its lowest conceivable level, and then lower it even more.

Add to the pot 1 large diced onion, 1 carrot cut in large pieces, or even 2, 1 large stick of celery, some parsley root, bay leaf, black peppercorns, allspice, and one clove. It's also nice to add the tail ends of some dill and cilantro. A cultured person always saves the leftovers from their herbs for soup.[5]

After about 40 minutes, add salt, remove the chicken, and strain the broth. You should rub the root vegetables on the strainer into the pot.

This is how to make a classic Jewish broth, which heals colds and brings simple gastronomic pleasures without excessive effort. Especially if you eat it with sweetish croutons. This is the broth that generations of Jews in all countries of the diaspora were raised on.

[1] This is a perfect example of the understated double negative that creates much of the irony and humor in Vail and Genis's style.

[2] The Jewish chicken broth the authors describe is quite similar to French consommé, but we don't need to confuse matters by bringing another ethnicity into the mix.

[3] Here, as is frequently the case, Vail and Genis choose vocabulary with a literary flavor. One needs *gramotnost'*, i.e., knowledge or expertise or culture or savvy, but the actual word means *literacy*. It seems that in the kitchen, as in writing, a person can improve himself along a skills trajectory, going from complete ignorance to basic literacy to the heights of artistic creation.

[4] Israel's southernmost city, Eilat is a port on the Red Sea.

[5] It's fun to construct a profile of a "cultured person" based on these essays—or to expand one's definition of "culture." Here cultured essentially means frugal.

One problem: You get sick of chicken. But then, there is beef broth, which can be doctored with various additions.

Russian tradition regards broth as an ingredient for making other dishes. For example, borscht. Jews see it as a self-contained culinary phenomenon.

For meat broth you need a good piece of boneless meat, about 5 pounds. Everything else, consult above. Except that you need to cook a beef broth for a long time (around 3 hours) and you can add a turnip to the root vegetables. When the soup is almost ready, you can change its flavor with minimal additions. For example, throw in just a couple of leaves of coarsely chopped cabbage. Red cabbage is better—it is spicier and produces the distinctive color of old Bordeaux. You can add sliced hotdogs, or smoked sausage, or ham, and generally anything you want.

It's hard to ruin a properly prepared broth.

People eat the meat boiled in the soup separately. And not only for economy's sake, but also because it is seen as a delicacy, so fine that you can even serve it for a holiday meal. It's eaten, naturally, with horseradish, and with clarified butter poured on it in great quantities.[6] Besides its tasty qualities, broth also possesses instructive merit: its clarity stands in contrast to our troubled times.

[6] You can make clarified butter by heating butter in a small saucepan over low heat for about 15 minutes. But you can also simply used melted butter here—the effect is similar.

CHAPTER 23

Salad and *Salo*[1]

[1] *Salo* becomes relevant in the last line of this chapter as being a truly Slavic food. In Russia or Ukraine, salted or smoked and cured slabs of backfat eaten on rye bread can accompany vodka and are seen as strength-giving. This is also an excellent way to preserve pork.

How do we differ from the French?

It's clear: our undeniable advantage is that they are frog-eaters. The Russian is a picky eater. He doesn't eat anything that jumps. But the Frenchman, in his flimsy little coat, with his little chicken mind, gobbles up everything laid before him.[1] Incidentally, the pragmatists who have infiltrated the Politburo have taken advantage of this fact. The Kostroma region, where crop and dairy yields have fallen sharply, fulfills its entire portion of the Gosplan by exporting frogs to France.[2] It's not for nothing that Andrei Voznesensky is proud of his Homeland:

> Trading for computers,
> Paris can appease.
> And in turn our frogs will gain
> Wide-reaching prestige.[3]

The usual arrangement is that you eat what you've got and you don't complain. But we have no intention of inciting our readers to consume amphibians (although they're not that bad stewed and slathered with a sauce of spicy mayonnaise). We understand the limits of the reader's culinary mettle. Instead we want to discuss the national food of the French. Not frogs (although that's where the people get their nickname), but salad.

A true French salad, funny though it seems, consists precisely and exclusively of salad [i.e., lettuce]. A few fresh, green leaves drizzled with dressing. Such food is so frivolous that Russians can't even conceive of it. When we say vegetable salad, we mean tomatoes, cucumbers, and all kinds of herbs, smothered with a healthy dose of sour cream.

But it won't do to reject salad greens altogether. It's possible to turn them into a delicious side dish. Boil 1 liter of water, throw in chopped lettuce (the dense romaine is best), bring the water back to a boil and then pour it off. In a pan, heat olive oil with 3 finely minced cloves of garlic for about 2 minutes. Add the lettuce and leave it over a medium flame for 3 to 4 minutes. Add salt and pepper.

Another side dish has even more pizzazz. Sauté a chopped green onion in olive oil for 2 to 3 minutes. Add chopped lettuce (raw). After a minute, add the juice of half of a lemon and half a teaspoon of sugar. When the lettuce starts to break down, move it to the edges of the pan and pour half a cup of cold cream in the center. After a minute, mix everything together, add salt, and use as a universal side dish to complement meat, fish, or chicken.

[1] The Russian for "flimsy" includes yet more gastronomical metaphors: a coat made of "fish fur," or scales, is completely unsuitable for Russian winters.

[2] *Gosplan* is one of the many abbreviations that infiltrated the Russian language during the Soviet period. It stands for the Russian phrase for State Planning Committee.

[3] Andrei Voznesensky (1933–2010) was a "child of the 1960s," a poet who was mentored by Boris Pasternak and called by American poet Robert Lowell "one of the greatest living poets in any language." The lines above appear in his 1983 poem "For Export."

As you see, even this simple green can be worthy if it's approached with Russian ingenuity. But to our minds a salad is generally its own special dish, of which even the clientele of "Health Food" stores can partake as much as they want. For example, the unforgettable *Salade Olivier*, a.k.a. "capital."[4] We shan't continue… Our hands tremble. We feel bittersweet tears welling up.

According to our observation, émigrés more and more often depart from traditional Russian salads under the influence of harmful "diet" propaganda. Insofar as our lifelong vocation is agreement and compromise, we want to offer a salad to satisfy the gourmet, the dieter, and the nostalgic alike. Its recipe is simple and delightful.

Mix 1 pound of crab meat (not canned; they'll have it premade in any decent fish shop) with 2 finely diced stalks of celery, 1.5 tablespoons of small capers, and the meat of 2 avocados (choose soft ones, so that you can dent them with your finger). Add a little pepper, but no salt. Add mayonnaise to taste and mix it all together.

Or try the Russian and Eastern versions of this dish. In the former, use 2 average-sized boiled potatoes instead of avocado; in the latter, 1 cup of steamed rice.

This is of course a concession, albeit a very tasty one, to the new, incorrect way of life, a substitute for the mighty Olivier, a.k.a. "capital," salad. But in our effort to comply, we would never lower ourselves so far as to serve up a plate of raw lettuce and try to pass it off as cooking.

From the Russian's point of view, such food is hollow, worthy of disdain. And there's some foundation to this judgment. Let's recall how the French, wearing our women's kerchiefs, fled the field of battle on paths paved with lettuce leaves in the face of our patriots, who in turn were bolstered by true ideology and sated by lard (cf. Lev Tolstoy, *Collection of Writings* in 20 volumes, Moscow, 1960, vol. 4–7).[5]

57

[4] The *Salade Olivier*, often referred to as *Stolichnyi salat* ("capital salad"), is a classic dish without which no Russian holiday can be celebrated—especially New Year's. On Olivier, see Anya von Bremzen, *Mastering the Art of Soviet Cooking*, chapter 7, and the recipe itself on pp. 316–17.

[5] I.e. *War and Peace*.

CHAPTER 24

Rehabilitating the Cutlet

Mincemeat cutlets are beloved, but not respected. They are desired, but not coveted. They are pleasant, but not prestigious. We can think of a whole list of things with similar characteristics: musical comedy, plump blondes, the detective novel.

There are fans of Julian Semyonov who will berate you in shrill, superior tones for never having read Prus's *In the Chateau with Young Girls in the Shower*.[1]

After the tenth shot, even a sophisticated connoisseur of jazz will start croaking out, "A white night and a bold, grey steed…"[2]

Those sensualists who blather on about long legs and flat bellies actually get excited when they see a body with (as they say back home) "something to hold on to."

And so forth. Our lives are governed by genuine passions, although it's customary to be ashamed of them. Or at least not to flaunt them.

Such epidemic duplicity is also on display in the sphere of gastronomy. If you ask someone who is partial to food about his culinary dispositions, his answer will repeat the menu at an expensive restaurant. And only this insincere gourmet's closest relatives know that he killed his brother for a skillet of cutlets with fried potatoes.

A potato is not a lobster: you can't take any pride in it. It's like when our grandfather comes to visit from the country. He gets up at six o'clock in the morning and sits around in his long johns loudly slurping tea. We can't really introduce him to our friends.[3]

Among our secret culinary pleasures, the mincemeat cutlet has a special place. Given the problems the meat industry faced back home, both in terms of quantity and quality, cutlets made up a good three quarters of the standard lunch menu. When run through a meat-grinder and flavored with spices, the final product could be considered high-quality. And there was lots of it.

This dish became so common that it lost the original adjective, "mincemeat."

We have forgotten that the word "cutlet" actually designates a piece of roasted meat with a bone in it. Indeed, what came to pass was a kind of linguistic sleight of hand: what was formerly a cutlet became known as a "chop steak" and then just a "chop." And its minced offspring took over the appellation "cutlet" completely.

So: the cutlet. For all its banality, it is an elegant and complex dish, which, alas, few can make properly. And all because of a lack of reverence, even though a well-made cutlet is so much richer and more delicious than a chop steak, a normal steak, or obviously a hamburger. You need only observe a few important rules that are often neglected due to the ubiquity of this dish.

[1] Julian Semenov (1931–93) was an investigative journalist and the founder of the International Association of Detective and Political Novels in the Soviet Union, but he is most famous for creating the character of Stierlitz, a "Soviet James Bond" (*Time* magazine). The adventures of this Soviet spy during World War II became the beloved twelve-part television movie *Seventeen Moments of Spring* (1973). Bolesław Prus (1847–1912) was a Polish author and philosopher. V&G here are joking at the expense of pseudo-literati, who might confuse Prus with Marcel Proust, or make an error citing the name of Proust's *In the Shadow of Young Girls in Flower* (volume 2 of *In Search of Lost Time*).

[2] A line from *The Serf Actress*, a 1963 musical film directed by Roman Tikhomirov. The film is set in the first years of the nineteenth century under Tsar Pavel I and is based on the operetta *Peasant Girl* by Soviet composer Nikolai Strelnikov.

[3] The above paragraphs seem more than usually random, a kind of stream-of-consciousness/free association prose, perhaps the linguistic version of running your ideas and reminiscences through a meatgrinder.

- Only ever make cutlets from freshly processed ground meat. Always use a meat grinder, never a food processor.
- It's best to combine meats. Use primarily beef (3/4 of the total), and add pork, lamb, or veal as you prefer.
- Add white bread soaked in milk (or water). Remove the crust.
- Add only the white of the egg, not the yolk. You need to separate the egg white and whip it well, then pour it into the mixture.

  It's up to you how to treat the onion. You can process a raw onion together with the meat, then the cutlets will be juicier. Or you can use finely diced and sautéed onion; that way the cutlets will have a more piquant, "fried" taste.

And that's all. But the main thing is to treat cutlets like a serious, responsible dish. Forget that they are served at every moldering cafeteria. After all, you can watch *Hamlet* at the House of Culture, but it plays at the Royal Shakespearean Theatre too.[4]

---

[4] Soviet "Houses of Culture" were generally attached to factories, collective farms, schools, and other organizations and were a kind of state-sponsored club where cultural and educational activities took place, including classes, concerts, plays, dances, meetings, etc.

CHAPTER 25

Adventures in Scent

Cuisine just begs to be compared to life. In both spheres, the aphorism is true: man eats to live, but does not live to eat. He actually lives to eat well.

If you compare everyday life to cold pasta, then it's easy to convince yourself: a little spice brings meaning to both. Love at first sight, tomato paste, a daring adventure, red pepper, the lottery, garlic.

But cuisine is more complicated than life: the list of spices is longer than the list of unusual events that might befall a regular person. Also, cuisine is more humane. No one has ever died from spices, which can't be said for adventures.

People who love spices lead exciting lives. They speculate in chrysanthemums, hijack airplanes, engage in blood feuds.[1] Nations that prefer raw foods are doomed to apathy and extinction. Take the Letts and the Samoyeds for starters.

Émigrés favor hot blood and a range of spices. A trip to Brighton Beach—with its mafia and Caucasian restaurants—is convincing enough. Still, how often we see people missing social cues and making culinary mistakes! There are so many who are incapable of distinguishing love from friendship or marjoram from caraway.

Even in the classic soup repertoire people are careless with their spices. And all you need to do is smash 10 black peppercorns and 1 allspice berry with the back of a spoon, break up 2 or 3 bay leaves, peel 2 to 3 cloves of garlic, and throw it all into a ready soup for the last 5 minutes before it's done (no earlier!). Child's play.

The degree to which émigrés are ignorant about their new life is even more criminal. What does the average émigré know about cardamom, star anise, or thyme? They may know everything about Kremlinology and mortgages, but about anise or wild basil—nothing.[2] It's a real shame.

The art of using spices is much like painting. There are basic correlations: blue sky, green grass, pink people. Or: rosemary goes with lamb, saffron with fish dishes, oregano with chicken, paprika with veal. But neither the painter nor the chef will get very far if they use only these cookie-cutter approaches. Here as nowhere else you need independence, creative audacity, and inspiration. Do you think you've got tips for Van Gogh?

Even the newcomer must be daring. Spices can make the most boring dish bright and festive, like a child's drawing or a painting by Pirosmani.[3]

[1] This collection of items references the Caucasus region, the most contentious part of the Russian Empire, Soviet Union, and Russian Federation. The region is known for its awe-inspiring natural beauty, the daring of its native population, and its resistance to Russian rule. In the twentieth and twenty-first centuries, the last of these has manifested in occasional acts of terrorism. The Caucasus is likewise the source of the spiciest dishes in Russian cuisine.

[2] The original uses "the old men in the Kremlin," a fixed expression that is commonly used in Russian émigré journalism.

[3] Niko Pirosmani (1862–1918) was a Georgian painter, generally referred to as a "naïve" artist belonging to the Primitivist movement, whose works focus on everyday themes with little attention paid to realistic portrayal. Pirosmani achieved fame shortly after his death, perhaps due to his idyllic depictions of life before World War I.

Take the omelet. It's as banal as an alarm clock. But pour together 3 eggs, 1/4 cup of cream, and 1 spoonful of carbonated water; add salt and fresh-ground black pepper (you shouldn't use other kinds at all, really). Beat in a tablespoon of dried basil and whip it to a froth with a whisk. Then lightly fry sliced tomato in oil, pour the mixture over it, and cook the omelet under a lid for about five minutes. While it's still in the pan, fold it in half and serve immediately. It will have a crisp crust on the outside and be semi-liquid in the middle, as it ought to be. A plate with this red-yellow-green omelet resembles a summer meadow filled with dandelions and poppies.

Spices must be everywhere and in everything. Add dried parsley to toast. Bake apples with cinnamon. Sprinkle boiled Brussels sprouts with nutmeg. And don't serve any seafood without at least an elementary sauce. Simmer finely minced garlic in melted butter and then cover generously with dried tarragon. Pour this sauce over boiled fish, prawns, or scallops, and that's all there is to it. French restaurants gladly charge exorbitant prices for this dish.

If you want to experiment with spices, cook big pieces of meat. It's hard to ruin them.

Let's take about a 3-4 pound beef tenderloin. We'll trim the fat and add all the basics. That is to say: garlic, a bay leaf, cloves (no more than 2 or 3), allspice, and black pepper. Then we'll rub the whole tenderloin with a blend of marjoram, caraway, and ginger. It's also not a bad idea to coat the meat with any non-Russian mustard.[4] Wrap it in foil and put it in the oven for about two hours. Salt the meat already at the table.

Incidentally, if you have an urge to add some other spices, don't hesitate. Flavor develops from dozens of ingredients, and only the chef himself knows what he put in. It's more interesting to live with spices than without. And how many things can you say that about in this world?

---

[4] Russian mustard is sharp and hot. Its high vinegar content may make it poorly suited for basting beef.

CHAPTER 26

The Wolf Is Fed and the Lamb Survives[1]

---

[1] "The wolf is fed and the lamb survives" is a Russian proverb that means something like "to have one's cake and eat it too."

A house with no soup is an unhappy one.[1] If everyone subsists on sandwiches, the family will collapse.[2] In our century, a century of existential loneliness, the most solid foundation is a pot of thick, hot soup. Young and old alike gather around to slurp down the rich fluid, chasing it with generous chunks of bread.[3]

A significant tradition of soup thrives only among certain kinds of peoples: those for whom poverty drives innovation. (In the western hemisphere, we've found, a predilection for soups exists only in the Caribbean islands, where this custom is left over from the time of slavery.)

Russian soup is a meal in and of itself. After a plate of properly prepared shchi, solyanka or rassolnik, it's hard even to get up from the table, let alone consider a main course.[4] And that's how it should be, especially in the winter.

But should we really withdraw into nationalistic narcissism? If we're carefully scrutinizing foreign life, shouldn't we turn our eyes to foreign dishes, too? We wonder: what's afloat in the free-form democratic soups brewed west of the Tisza?[5]

Vegetables.

There it is: the principal difference between East and West. For us, vegetables belong in a thick meat broth, but their vegetables swim about freely in a thin liquid. However, we shouldn't reject foreign practice out of hand. Vegetable soup is not so much about filling your belly, but rather experiencing pleasure. If you can bring the subtle essence of the vegetable to the table, then the reward will be in the aroma and the tender flavor, in the elegant delicacy and even (so they say) in the vitamins. Moreover, the only way to make shchi is to start in the morning, as soon as your wife leaves for work. But a vegetable soup is ready in half an hour. You can make it in your free time (as if you had anything else to do).

Besides, you don't need to follow a strict recipe for a vegetable soup. It is unfettered, like free verse. But, like free verse, it requires good taste and common sense.

Let's take, for instance, a head of cauliflower. Cut it up into florets and put them in salted boiling water. As soon as the water comes back to a boil, add 2 tablespoons of cream of wheat. After about 15 minutes, the cauliflower will have softened. Add 2 cups of milk and as much butter as you're willing to part with. And that's all. Once it's in the bowl, sprinkle parsley and grated cheese on top. Of course, it's no Ukrainian borscht, but it's not bad. The main thing is that even if they're obsessed with dieting, your wives and daughters will like it.

Or try this spinach soup. You don't have to think of spinach as cow fodder. You can chop it finely and throw it in a pan with melted butter, add diced scallions and salt, and sweat the spinach until the pile of greens becomes a kind of brown slurry. Then pour in 1 liter of boiling water and add a handful of pasta. As soon as the pasta is cooked,

[1] Here V&G refer to the famous opening line of Tolstoy's novel *Anna Karenina*: "All happy families are alike; each unhappy family is unhappy in its own way."

[2] Here again the *buterbrod*, the open-faced sandwich called *Butterbrot* in German. For Russians, the idea of dining on something cold is anathema. Eating dry and cold food conjures up privation and evokes the dry rations or bagged lunch of a military or other institutional feeding regime.

[3] This expression in English usually means to chase with liquid, but in Russia you never drink anything without taking a bite of something. See comments on drinking traditions in chapter 29 note 2 and in chapter 39.

[4] On these soups see chapters 3, 6, and 29.

[5] The river Tisza divided the territory of the USSR from Europe.

add 1 cup of milk to the soup. Chop a hard-boiled egg into the bowl before pouring in the soup, then sprinkle with grated *bryndza* cheese (2 tablespoons per portion).[6] Now you have made a classic Bulgarian dish, and as you know the Bulgarians are famed not only for their devotion to socialism, but also for their longevity.

Or try making a "compromise soup." The main thing you need for this recipe is imagination, since this soup permits any vegetables at all. Let's take red cabbage as the base. It brings a spicy flavor and a vivid color. We'll dice up a small head (of cabbage please—no murder in the kitchen!), throw it into boiling water, and then let our fancy take over. We can add yellow or green onion, turnips or carrots, potatoes or celery, parsley root or tomatoes. Maybe all of them, as long as the soup doesn't get too thick. When the soup has simmered for about 10 minutes, put in some chopped smoked sausage or *myśliwska* (big or small chunks).[7] After about another 10 minutes, flavor the soup with a bay leaf, black pepper, garlic, and any herb: parsley, dill, celery. And that's all. This is neither meat nor vegetable soup, but it's tasty. Besides, you have relieved the refrigerator of leftovers.

It shouldn't be supposed that people who make vegetable soup do it out of poverty or parsimony. They do it out of intellectual curiosity.

[6] Bryndza is a sheep's milk cheese, similar to feta, made in Poland, Ukraine, and Slovakia.

[7] *Myśliwska*, a Polish hunter's sausage, is also available in Ukraine. Lightly smoked and dried, it is usually made of pork, though it may include beef, plus salt, pepper, and juniper. The name derives from its nonperishability, which makes it ideal for hunters and for other outdoor expeditions such as hiking, fishing, or camping.

CHAPTER 27

Pelmeni for the Lazy

МОСКОВСКИЙ
ОРДЕНА ЛЕНИНА
МЯСОКОМБИНАТ

Laziness will be the death of émigré culture. Despicable laziness and its nasty consequence—a preference for seeking an easy way out. Thank God they don't let our people into the sphere of politics, where our habit of hasty shortcuts could have serious effects: resolving the Middle East situation with a nuclear bomb, dealing with crime through mass public executions, and so on. All of these solutions derive from laziness. Why was Ilya Muromets such a fine heroic fellow?[1] Because he sat on a stove for three and thirty years and got used to being lazy. So when he finally climbed down from the stove, it was easier to chop off a stranger's head than to undertake the unaccustomed effort of diplomatic finesse and mutual understanding.

But forget politics. We're not welcome there—and we shouldn't be. We are, however, welcome to approach the stove without any limitations: "democracy," don't you know. And here, the émigré inclination to primitive laziness inflicts serious damage on the Russian cultural heritage which we brought with us abroad. All is forgotten: grandfather's recipes, mother's instructions, and the wisdom of the ages.

Our grief is not without reason. For example, let's take the pride of the Russian table—pelmeni.[2] The availability and affordability of this dish made it one of the most common in our homeland. In the first years after arriving, pelmeni brought joy to émigré tables. But time passed, and our homes went into decline. Now, many prefer Chinese dumplings to pelmeni, and the especially perverse go for Italian ravioli and tortellini. Even those who still believe in tradition buy pelmeni ready-made—forgetting that store-bought pelmeni are stamped out by a soulless machine, a device incapable of love or passion.

It's not our task to correct our compatriots, but rather to help them find a compromise. So we call upon them to learn to prepare something that basically looks like pelmeni, but is simpler to prepare and no less tasty. In short—pelmeni for the lazy.

This recipe was invented by people in the East, where the climate is seductively warm and the people didn't suffer our long, dark winters. During those winters we punched out thousands of pelmeni. The whole family would get together and make a lifetime supply. Only northern peoples like us are capable of such quiet dumb heroics. (By the way, pelmeni, contrary to popular belief, are not Siberian, but a dish from Perm. So Perm is famed for more than just dinosaur fossils and the ballerina Nadya Pavlova.[3])

[1] Ilya Muromets is a folk hero in the tradition of the *bogatyrs* (similar to the Western knights errant). According to legend, he was sickly in his youth and spent his first three decades immobile on the Russian stove (see note, chapter 3). He was miraculously healed (by a beggar? Or pilgrims? Legends contradict each other) and shortly thereafter began legendary feats of strength and daring.

[2] Every culture has dumplings, and *pelmeni* are the Russian form of this filling and comforting food.

[3] Perm is a city and administrative district in the Ural Mountains. Robert Murchison and Edouard de Verneuil conducted foundational geological research there, resulting in Murchison's naming the Permian Period after the region. Nadezhda Pavlova was indeed a famous ballerina who performed in Perm, but our authors neglect perhaps the most famous ballet impresario in history: Sergei Diaghilev, founder of the Ballets Russes in Paris, who spent his early years in Perm.

Eastern "pelmeni" differ from northern ones first of all in size. The thick dough (made of flour, eggs, salt, water) is rolled out and cut into squares (about 10 by 10 centimeters), such that 6 or 7 make enough for 1 portion. Obviously, shaping them takes much less effort. After adding the filling (1.5 tablespoons) the dough is twisted at the top in a knot that doesn't cook through and isn't supposed to: Those eating hold on to this knot, but do not eat it.

Georgian *khinkali* begin with 4 parts ground lamb and 1 part ground beef. To the meat, add diced onion, cilantro, garlic, red pepper, and salt. Boil the khinkali with vegetable roots in a large pot of salted water, enough so there is room for the khinkali to move about.

Armenian *boreks* are filled with ground beef, onion, parsley, dill, black pepper, and salt. First, the filling is browned in a pan. The molded boreks are dropped into water until they are partially cooked, then fried up in a pan.

Uzbek *manty* are steamed in a "stimer" [steamer] which is easily accessible in the West: either a bamboo Chinese version or a metal European one. Manty are made with cubed lamb, onion, black pepper, caraway seeds, salt, and small pieces of lamb fat—one slice of fat per dumpling. The steamer pan should be lightly greased with butter or oil. Cooking by steam takes 40 to 45 minutes.

Turkmen *balik berek* are the same as manty, except filled with fish. Fish fillets are cut into small cubes, dressed with a raw egg, and mixed with onion, dill, parsley, salt, and a pinch each of red pepper and cardamom.

And so, if we exchange northern pelmeni for their eastern relatives, then maybe we will earn the right to call our laziness luxury. And that's a completely different matter.

69

CHAPTER 28

Aristocrats
in a Can

"When you go to tie your tie, take the utmost care. With the redfish, after all, one color does it share." With this little couplet Vagrich Bakhchanyan—a moralist with an acid wit—taught our children well.[1] Or not so well. By redfish, he had in mind that crimson salmon famously served at Kremlin banquets. But here the native of the Caucasus was led astray by his ignorance of Russian life. Real patriots write the following: "Although their meat is white, the fish of the sturgeon family (*ossetra, sevruga, beluga, shipa, sterlet, kaluga*) were known in times of old as 'redfish.' The term 'redfish' was given to sturgeon in the ancient sense of the word 'red' meaning something rare, expensive, and beautiful. Maidens were 'red' (*krasna-devitsa*) as was the sun (*krasnoe solnyshko*) and even valuable goods (*krasnyi tovar*)." (*A Book about Tasty and Healthy Food*.[2] Yes, you know the one.)

In emigration, of course, there is neither Kaluga[3] nor *kaluga*, to say nothing of sterlet. Among fabulous fishes only salmon remains.

But instead of grieving over the irretrievable loss of beluga, it's better to become familiar with the bounty of salmon in our new hemisphere. It's worth it, and not just for the lox. Smoked salmon needs neither praise nor preparation. You squirt the pink meat with a little lemon and eat it up—that's all there is to it.

Raw salmon needs more skillful treatment. The problem is that salmon, like any aristocrat, suffers from an inherent dryness. To ameliorate this flaw the utmost tact is required. Don't just stick a salmon fillet into a pan like they do in fancy (but deranged) American restaurants. You must approach the process with compassion, and keep your wits about you.

Place a piece of the fillet, enough for one portion, on some aluminum foil. Pour lemon juice over the fish and add a few pieces of onion, carrot shavings, salt, and a dab of butter. Then carefully fold the foil into a packet and put it in the oven for half an hour. No less, but especially no more. It needs to be eaten immediately; straight out of the foil adds a certain panache.

The trick here is to keep the precious juice from draining out of its foil packet. That's what keeps the salmon moist. Just as the bartender lubricates the dry society at an aristocratic reception (though of course we've never quite made the guest list).

But there are easier ways. Canned salmon, for example—now that's a poor man's luxury. On the one hand the Russian despises canned foods, but on the other hand he delights in them. The confusion is because both sprats in tomato sauce and fine, lightly salted caviar come in tins. Regardless, we tend to see canned food as a finished product, which makes a chef of anyone with a can opener.

Canned salmon, though, is an inexpensive, convenient processed food with great potential.[4]

[1] Vagrich Bakhchanyan (1938–2009) was an artist and poet who emigrated to NYC about the same time as V&G and collaborated with them. He designed the cover to the first edition of this book.

[2] *A Book about Tasty and Healthy Food* (first edition 1939) was the official treatise on food preparation by the Institute of Nutrition of the Academy of Medical Scientists of the USSR. Its aim was to create a modern, scientific alternative to Molokhovets' *A Gift to Young Housewives*. See note in chapter 14 on Elena Molokhovets.

[3] Kaluga is an ancient Russian city southwest of Moscow.

[4] The Russian is *polufabrikat*, literally "half-fabrication." The term encompasses frozen and pre-prepared meals, and we have translated it either as "processed foods" or in terms of progress toward a completed dish: "you're halfway there."

Easiest is to make it into fish soup. Just throw potatoes, carrots, onion, parsley root, and a bay leaf into some water and after 20 minutes add green peas, salmon, a tablespoon of butter, salt, fresh-ground pepper, and herbs. A resourceful fellow will also put in a tomato, sour cream, grated cheese, or something else. Just like Pasternak, this soup exudes simplicity and nobility, both of which he had in spades.[5]

And then there's salmon soufflé, which like everything delicate comes from the West. Whisk 4 egg yolks into 1/2 pound of hot mashed potatoes. Mix this with the crumbled contents of one can of salmon. Add a finely diced onion, a little bit of bell pepper, 1/4 cup of milk, and salt and pepper. Mix until it becomes a homogenous mass, then lay it in a soufflé dish and smooth and brush the surface with the whipped whites of those four eggs you cracked before. After about 25 minutes, take your soufflé out of the oven and serve with white wine and well-earned pride.

You can actually make an entire meal—appetizer, soup, and main course—from salmon. Only don't get it in your mind to try. Your guests won't understand.

[5] See Pasternak's 1931 poem "Waves" (*Volny*):

> Assured of kinship with all things
> And with the future closely knit,
> We can't but fall—a heresy!—
> To unbelievable simplicity.
>
> Never doubting the kinship among all that is,
> Or the present and future's complicity,
> We are drawn in the end to the curious sin,
> Of unheard of, unrivalled simplicity.

Two translations, by George Reavey (1959) and Thomas Feerick (2017). Reavey's translation, like Pasternak's original poem, uses iambic tetrameter; Feerick has created a similar wave-like effect using anapests.

The Russian *Rassole*

Let's render unto Caesar what is Caesar's. The English can have Sherlock Holmes and Parliament; the French can have love and musketeers; the Americans—democracy and Hollywood. But let Russia pride itself on its ballet and pickles.

In the States they have long loved Russian ballet, and yet real pickled cucumbers are hard to come by. Which makes sense: a pickle is not Baryshnikov; you can't put it on television.[1]

But we are offended nonetheless. After all, we've been pickling cucumbers in Rus' since the twelfth century. And neither the Tatars, nor the Poles, nor the Bolsheviks could break the people of this remarkable habit. Especially since pickles have often been the only zakuska available.

Still, pickles are not just for snacking. (In a pinch you can chase with textiles.)[2] Pickled cucumbers are an essential and irreplaceable ingredient of many Russian dishes, for example solyanka, *rassolnik*, *kalya*, Tatar *azu*, and the Olivier salad.

---

[1] The ballet dancer, choreographer, and actor Mikhail Baryshnikov (b. 1948) defected to Canada in 1974, leaving the Leningrad Kirov Ballet company to eventually work with George Ballanchine at the New York City Ballet, and at the American Ballet Theatre, where he became artistic director. His roles in films such as *The Turning Point* (1977) made him a household name in late-twentieth-century United States.

---

[2] Here we must take into account the specificities of the *zakuska*. Although appetizers are part of many national cuisines, in Russia they have an extra function—Russians never drink alcohol without nibbling something afterward, the reverse of "washing it down." At the same time, there isn't always food available when you want a drink, so other habits have formed, such as sniffing your wrist after a shot to help it go down. The reference here to *manufaktura*, or dry goods, textiles, must be in this vein: in a desperate situation you can sniff your sleeve as a "chaser" to an alcoholic drink.

If the above leads readers to think they are about to get a recipe for pickling cucumbers here, they shouldn't get their hopes up. To make pickles, you need a wooden tub, juniper branches, a hut with a cellar, and superstitions (it is a widely known fact that you mustn't pickle anything under a full moon).

However, in America you can certainly buy pickles. They are sold by Jews who brought this culinary secret from the same country as we did, just earlier. But be careful they don't try to foist a surrogate on you instead—a kosher dill pickle.[3] Such things do happen, and the result is lamentable.

But if you have managed to secure real pickled cucumbers, make a *rassolnik*. You won't regret it. This is a national soup, like the *khorovod* is a national dance.[4] It's truly a food of the people—of the peasants, even.

First of all, forget all of the cafeteria associations you've formed of the proud but compromised dish "rassolnik." Once you've forgotten, tackle the meat byproducts. They are the essence of rassolnik, and in them lies its strength.

You should boil the nearly odorless beef kidneys they sell in sterile America for about five minutes. Then mercilessly remove any bits you find suspicious and chop the kidneys directly into the pot.

[3] Marinated cucumbers are what we call "pickled," while salted cucumbers are sometimes referred to as "half-sour pickles."

[4] The *khorovod* is a traditional Slavic circle dance, performed by groups of women during festivals, more often than not in summertime.

[5] The name *rassolnik*, of course, comes from *rassole*, which means pickling juice. This liquid is cherished in some Russian households, not just for the soup one can make, but also as a hangover cure.

Boil some tongue (veal is best) until it's halfway cooked, then pop it under cold water and remove the skin. The skin should slip off easily and sensuously, like a stocking sliding off a girl's leg. Pour the broth with the chopped tongue into the pot with the kidneys, add boiling water, and simmer for half an hour.

In the meantime prepare the other ingredients, for the rassolnik demands it. Wash 2 tablespoons of pearl barley in cold water, pour boiling water over it, cover, and let it steam. Cut up your pickles with appropriate reverence and boil them in their own rassole for about 10 minutes, skimming the foam all the while.[5] Cut a carrot into matchsticks, chop some parsley and celery, and cube a potato. Now you need to bring everything together, but even this must be done with discernment. First, throw the roots and grains into the soup. After 10 minutes, add the potato and two chopped onions. Add the pickles with their rassole only when everything has been cooked (otherwise the water will be too acidic, and the potato will harden). It's best not to salt the soup at all. Instead, just add a little more rassole.

Three minutes before it is ready, add chopped dill, parsley, celery, 3 laurel leaves, 6 black peppercorns, and 2 allspice berries. Then turn off the gas, cover with the lid, and wait while the soup comes together, if you have the patience.

Of course, rassolnik must be eaten with sour cream and black bread, but what must be cherished is the broth, which unites a measured acidity with the hearty aroma of giblets.

You can make a simpler (but worse) rassolnik with poultry (duck is best). Carve the giblets up into little bits: the stomach (or belly, as we call it), heart, liver, and neck. Pour fresh boiling water over it all, and cook for an hour. Everything else—as above. Except you can use rice instead of pearl barley, and add garlic and tarragon to the list of spices.

You can also make a fish rassolnik, which is difficult, or a vegetarian one, which is silly. The only ingredient you can't do without is pickles. But then without them, everything in emigration is hard.

74

CHAPTER 30

Borscht, with a Side of Emancipation

It's well known that women don't eat. They just peck at this or that. No wonder they are disinclined to waste their lives on the bottomless pits known as men.

Throughout the twentieth century, women have sought to be free from kitchen slavery—from kettles, pots, and dirty dishes; from borscht, cutlets, and *kompot*; from bouillabaisse, lobsters, and meringues; at the end of the day they sought freedom from their hungry husbands.

They succeeded, they broke free, they escaped their servitude.[1] Now housewives are found only in museums, where they stand between the dinosaurs and the first airplane.

But since a holy place never remains empty (and a kitchen undoubtedly is one such place), men stepped up to the stovetop. Today no one is surprised by a female rabbi, female soccer player, or female general. But just try to find a female cook in a good restaurant!

One need only eavesdrop on our ladies' conversation in order to understand how far emancipation has come. "Whom do you prefer, George Sand or Jane Fonda?"—"I'd say Reagan is more to my liking."[2] Men chatter about entirely different topics: "Did I hear you right, you put apple in your *forshmak*?"

It's not that men and women have exchanged places. Instead, they changed the very places themselves. If for a woman the kitchen is hell, then for a man it's a temple. Where a woman labored, a man performs holy rites. For one it's bondage, for the other it's a passion.

While the weaker sex struggles to become stronger, men collect stamps, walk poodles, and pickle cucumbers.

It requires great skill to avoid responsibilities.[3] Women have escaped their duty to be good wives, and now with a light heart they can earn money, run for president, or study karate. Men in turn have shouldered the burden of culinary knowledge. To each his own.

The amazing thing is that everyone is satisfied. Women thrive on their careers and their starvation diets, while men write cookbooks. Most curious of all is that kitchen labor—denigrated for centuries—turns out to be no worse than any other work. It's even somewhat better. It's all about the poetry.

Can you really find poetry in peeling potatoes? You can if you know that your every movement is a conscious step toward the creation of a culinary masterpiece. Renaissance artists ground their own paints. They saw in this mechanical procedure the foundation of future Mona Lisas.

Each chef strives to achieve a harmony in which nothing seems excessive, insignificant, or boring. That is to say, when you're cutting carrots, you're doing far more than that: you are releasing the vital flavor and color components of borscht.

[1] In Russian this is a three-word sentence, three perfective past tense verbs, which brings to mind such classic rhetorical phrases as "Veni, vidi, vici." In fact, the entire chapter is built on threes—see the description of woman's kitchen slavery above, or the comparison between women and men's attitudes toward the kitchen a few paragraphs later.

[2] George Sand was the pen name of the French novelist Amantine Lucile Aurore Dupin (1804–76). Her importance for Russian ideas of emancipation cannot be exaggerated, but the reference looks particularly amusing in conjunction with Jane Fonda (b. 1937), the American actress and political activist known for her anti-Vietnam War stance but who by 1982 had become more famous for her exercise videos for women. These women's interest in President Ronald Reagan (1911–2004) implies that they have moved out of purely female spheres into the world of big politics.

[3] In Russian this is "great art," possibly a reference to works by Cardano (mathematics) and Llull (philosophy/logic) in the medieval and Renaissance periods. Cardano's work features the first application of imaginary numbers, and Llull's provides foundational logical mechanisms much admired and implemented by Gottfried Leibniz, a contemporary (and sometimes rival) of Sir Isaac Newton.

The issue is gender psychology. When a woman prepares borscht, she does so with internal (and sometimes even external) tears. For her it's a symbol of age-old enslavement, and while preparing borscht she laments her desecrated childhood, lost youth, and untimely aging. Woman is shackled to borscht. And sooner or later, she realizes that she has nothing to lose but her chains.[4]

Men approach borscht as dilettantes, as amateurs. Nonprofessionals take a peculiar, creative interest in other people's business. And that's why for men borscht is a matter of pride rather than humiliation.

In any case, this is how we see our reader. A humble, toiling intellectual, always ready to experiment. After all, if cookbooks were written only for the modern woman, the recipes would read: Open a can of soup, thaw a meat patty, wash it all down with Pepsi-Cola, and go to a karate lesson.

[4] An echo of the call for a worker's rebellion from *The Communist Manifesto*, by Marx and Engels, "The Proletarians have nothing to lose but their chains." Interestingly, Marx and Engels' famous conclusion, "Workers of the world, unite!" was originally penned by a woman, Flora Tristan (*The Workers' Union*, 1843), five years before the *Manifesto* was published. Another example of men taking over for women?

The potato, if nothing else, was a recurrent food in our Russian diet. Basically, we ate them every day.[2] And so we settled into a familiar relationship with the potato. It's like the way you feel about a close relative who never really made it: Love doesn't preclude condescension.

No matter what they say, blood ties are the most enduring.

Of course, we're not the only ones who claim the potato. Meals wouldn't be the same without it in England, France, or America either. The Germans have a special reverence for the potato, serving it whole, still in the skin, and they savor every morsel.

But Russian cooking has worked out a truly meticulous approach to the potato. We don't just boil potatoes, we transform them into a culinarily complete and independent course. To that end, we slather the cooked potato with tons of butter, toss some fresh dill on top, and eat it very hot with a half-sour pickle. Not bad, eh?

When making a purée, Russians spare no effort in mashing the potato so they won't be left with lumps. At the same time, you must constantly pour hot milk and butter into the purée. After adding a couple spoonfuls of sour cream or whipped egg whites, you can achieve

---

[2] In the post-Soviet world, the potato became a marker of fortitude and tenacity. See Nancy Ries, "Potato Ontology: Surviving Post-Socialism in Russia," *Cultural Anthropology* 24, no. 2 (2009): 181–212.

CHAPTER 31

A Relative in a Military Jacket[1]

---

[1] Baked potatoes are called "potatoes in their jackets" in Russian.

such an airy texture that it would be a shame to use it as a side dish. And there's no need. The potato is lovely in the nude. Not every woman can make that claim.

For those who don't agree with these daring comments, we suggest adding some grated carrot, or spinach, or a beet to the purée. Elemental Futurists would surely love the contrasting colors of this dish.[3]

Every émigré knows that Hanukkah means latkes. But that doesn't mean you can't eat latkes every day. It doesn't take a rabbi to make them. Shred a raw potato on your finest grater, add a little flour and, with a spoon as your ladle, fry the mixture in butter. Latkes are good with *gribenes*.[4] No need to explain how to make gribenes. If you know what Hanukkah means, then you know how to make gribenes. And if you don't know, have your latkes with sour cream.

In our view, the very best of the best—what culinary fantasy combined with experience can produce—is fried potatoes. Of course, we're not talking about that pathetic, crunchy surrogate, "french fries," which we used to call "straw" back home.[5] No, like any masterpiece, genuine fried potatoes require 99% effort and 1% talent. Most of humanity is certain that they will get by with the opposite ratio.

Cut a potato into strips (neither thick nor thin). Fry them covered (at first) and uncovered (at the end). Stir them frequently, but with a gentle touch. Somewhere in the middle of the process, add raw onion and a bay leaf, and maybe a little garlic. And then, when the whole pan is suffused with a healthy yellow-brown glow, serve up the fried potatoes with sour cream. It is delicious, but complicated. So we make no guarantees.

Potato skins are simpler and more exotic. No matter how poor we were in Russia, we never sank so far as to eat potato skins.[6] But here they serve them in the best restaurants without a second thought. And they're not bad.

Thoroughly wash a potato, [bake it,] then scoop it out and throw the skin into boiling oil. After about five minutes, take the skin out and let it dry on a paper towel. Add salt and eat with whatever comes to mind. For example, with beer. Then you can write home to Russia that we're eating potato scraps here, which explains why you still haven't sent the fur coat you promised.

[3] Futurism was an artistic school in prerevolutionary Russia, the most vivid representatives of which were David Burliuk, Vladimir Mayakovsky, and Kazimir Malevich. Art forms included poetry and visual arts, especially books and posters, and their works often featured bold primary colors. There were many kinds of futurists (cubo-futurists, ego-futurists, etc.), but "elemental futurists" is V&G's own term. Since the Russian word for elemental (*stikhiinyi*) seems etymologically close to the word for poetry (*stikhi*), the question arises: Can one be an elemental futurist *without* being a poet?!

[4] *Gribenes* are a kosher equivalent of pork rinds. Chicken or goose skin is fried in the rendered fat (schmaltz) of the same animal.

[5] Similar to American shoestring fries, Russian "potato straws" are sold now in bags like potato chips.

[6] Soviet citizens believed—and not without reason—that the skins of vegetables needed to be removed so as to avoid the poisons of chemicals and fertilizers.

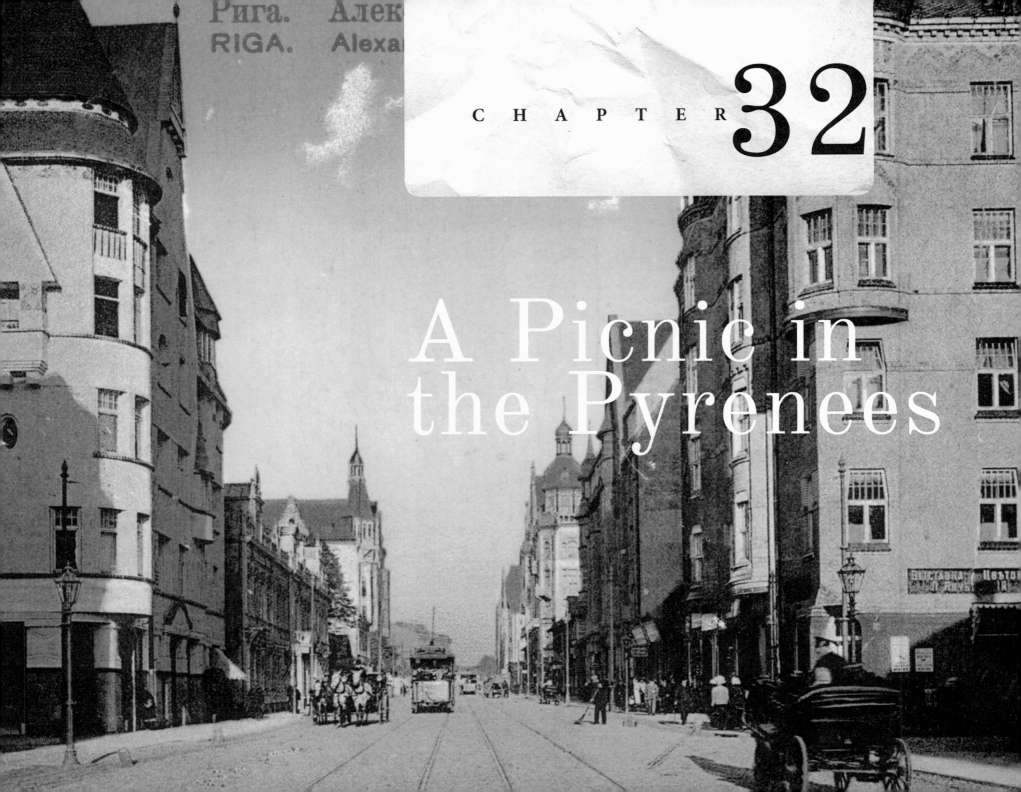

CHAPTER 32

A Picnic in
the Pyrenees

Landing in the West, an émigré first satisfies his passion for all things formerly unavailable: He opens newspapers and restaurants, feasts his eyes on black people, becomes a Jew, travels to the Bahamas.

Once settled, the émigré begins to practice in his new land all his old familiar habits: in the newspapers he praises the government, in restaurants he shortchanges the clientele and sings "Red Flower," he avoids Jews, calls black people "miners," and longs for Gurzuf.[1] In addition to the vast supply of collective memories, each émigré has his own private ones. Our friend the artist became ecstatic when he read in the Guinness Book of World Records that the largest prison in the entire world is located in his hometown of Kharkov.

As for us, we are hopeless: we're from Riga. Everywhere we go, with a schizophrenic singlemindedness we seek brick barns and Gothic cathedrals.[2] For us, lancet windows are the sanctuary of human genius, and, with apologies to Michelangelo, we simply prefer Germany to Italy.

Despite this particular geographic characteristic, we are still Russians, and so are delighted to identify the landscapes of Valdai in Quebec, the bridges of Leningrad in London, and the racket of Odessa in Naples.

However, there is no country in Europe or America which resembles Russia more than Spain. Framing the cultural European continent from the west and east, in the Middle Ages both the Spaniards and the Russians suffered crippling blows, falling under the yokes of the Moors and the Mongols for centuries. Civilization came to these borderlands later than to the rest of the Western world, but it's not our culinary business to expound on historical themes. We will only note that on the streets of Madrid we are always being pulled up short at the sight of a familiar person, one of us, and it wouldn't surprise us in the least if a passerby suddenly started speaking Russian. Even the language, with its clear phonetics, sounds like ours. Nothing evokes such feelings of protest and alienation as the speech habits of other peoples: those guttural sounds of the French, the lisping of Poles, the rapid tongue-twisting of Italians.

Spaniards speak slowly, with gravitas—the way our guys hold forth outside a liquor store. In Spain no one rushes around as they do in New York, but they also don't spend all day napping like in Greece. Spanish men stand in groups on the corner, legs spread, dressed in white shirts with the sleeves rolled up and loosely hanging bell-bottom trousers, belts resting gently on their … well, below their bellies. A real Spaniard is slightly tipsy and always ready for a drink. And a snack—and he's not particularly finicky.

There is a certain coarseness to Spanish cuisine, which is common among nations late to recognize cuisine as a high art. The French and the Italians inherited Roman refinement, while we and the Spaniards were engaging in hand-to-hand combat with the Moors and Tatars for your freedom and ours. Even later on we shared something in the military vein: See Svetlov's poem "Grenada," "¡No pasaran!", or Agustín Gómez—captain of "Torpedo" … In brief, where did the boy get that Spanish melancholy?![3]

Not considering cooking a serious enterprise, Spaniards threw everything into a big heap and only took care with the quality of the initial ingredients. This romantic eclectic of

[1] "Red Flower" is a popular Ukrainain folk song. Gurzuf is a resort town on the Crimean peninsula, coincidentally, perhaps, the place where Anton Chekhov had his dacha.

[2] Russian dissidents had a special relationship to psychiatric diagnoses, particularly schizophrenia, since the label of "sluggish schizophrenia" was frequently used to imprison dissidents indefinitely in Soviet mental hospitals. For more, see Bloch and Reddaway, *Russia's Political Hospitals* (1977).

[3] This phrase, "where did the boy get that Spanish melancholy," is a quote from Mikhail Svetlov's 1926 poem "Granada." "¡No pasaran!" ("They shall not pass!") is a phrase from the Spanish Civil war, while Agustin Gomez was a Spanish Communist leader and captain of the Moscow soccer team "Torpedo." He is buried in Donskoi cemetery in Moscow.

Spanish cuisine is perfect for busy people, of whom there are so many among us émigrés. After all, we are conquering America! At the same time Spanish dishes are spicy, pungent, and quite presentable.

For example, paella. It's easy to make and delicious to eat.

There are many kinds of paella. The most festive of them is paella *mariscada*.

добавить две чашки (!) мелко нарезанной петрушки, влить немного оливкового масла, всыпать нарезанный чеснок (8-10 зубчиков). Уложить поверх предварительно слегка отваренные креветки, сырые скаллопсы, кусочки сырого рыбного филе, готовое мясо крабов. Обильно посыпать все эстрагоном. Заранее приготовить мидии (mussels). Дюжины две мидий бросить на горячую сковороду, слегка смазанную маслом, и дождаться, когда створки откроются и выпустят сок. Все вместе — раковины и сок высыпать на остальной seafood в кастрюлю, добавить, если надо, бульон из-под креветок и потушить минут пять.

Отдельно отварить рис — обязательно с красным перцем, щепоткой мускатного ореха и шафраном.

Выложить готовый рис на большое блюдо, сверху — содержимое кастрюли. Пропитанный соками морских тварей, пряный рис в сочетании с самими тварями украсит жизнь. Под паэлью марискаду хорошо идут ария Кармен, арагонская хота, танец падеспань и русский национальный напиток водка.

In a wide, flat pan sauté finely diced onion and celery in oil. Then add 2 cups (!) finely diced parsley, pour in a little olive oil, and sprinkle in minced garlic (8–10 cloves). Place on top lightly boiled shrimp, raw scallops, a raw, cubed fish fillet, and prepared crabmeat. Sprinkle generously with tarragon. Prepare the mussels in advance. Throw about 2 dozen mussels into a hot, lightly oiled frying pan, and wait until they hinge open to release their juices. Toss everything, together with the shells and juices, onto the rest of the seafood in the pan, add, if necessary, the shrimp cooking water, and simmer for about 5 minutes.

Cook the rice separately with red pepper, a pinch of nutmeg, and some saffron.

Arrange the prepared rice onto a large dish and pour the contents of the pan over it. This spicy rice soaked in seafood juices, along with the seafood itself, will enhance your life. Pair the paella mariscada with the aria from *Carmen*, an Aragón *jota*, the dance *pas d'Espagne*, and the Russian national drink—vodka.[4]

---

[4] This seemingly eclectic mix of Spanish cultural motifs merely serves to underline the point about the connections between the two nations. Everything here has ties to Russia: The novella on which Bizet's *Carmen* was based was written by Prosper Merimée, a Frenchman who also translated Pushkin, Gogol, and Turgenev; in 1845 Mikhail Glinka composed an aragonese *jota*—his first "major" orchestral piece after adapting Pushkin's narrative poem *Ruslan and Liudmila* for opera; and the *pas d'Espagne* was written and choreographed by Russian ballet master Alexander Alexandrovich Tsarman in 1901. Tsarman was also known for dancing the role of Don Quixote at the Bolshoi Theater; he, like our authors, loved the exotic, and composed dances such as the "ball *czardas*," "ball *lezginka*," tarantella, and Ukrainian "*kozachok*." Note that in chapter 2 V&G refer to tea as the *other* Russian national drink.

CHAPTER 33

Exotic and Stinky

In Russia, the cheese department was the most exotic part of the grocery. In some strange way there was always cheese present, and yet it seemed to be utterly absent.

Everything periodically disappeared from the shops. Even pasta—and this was in peacetime! But like the bust of the leader, cheese was a constant.

One time we were in Naro-Fominsk and decided to check out the food store near the station.[1] The saleswoman dozed dully and the radio played: "Today you did not bring me a bouquet of lush roses ..."[2] In terms of edibles there was only a single gray cube with the label "Rot-Front Cheese," chopped from a larger hunk.[3] And nothing else. No tulips, no lilies.

So there was cheese. But really, there wasn't. With asparagus and lobsters the case is more or less clear: They do not occur naturally in the Valdai Hills. But cheese was actually produced, if somewhat later than in the rest of Europe. True, Homer and Aristotle were already writing about cheese, while in our country the first cheese dairies appeared only after the abolition of serfdom. This is new evidence in favor of democracy. Apparently the same bacteria yield both cheese and civil liberties. But regardless, the only well-known cheese dish in our country was the cheese sandwich.

It's a shame, because there are fine cheeses in Russia. We are not talking about the unforgettable processed cheese, the joy of Russian drunks: that is a sociological phenomenon, not a culinary one.[4] Brine cheeses (feta, *suluguni*, and *chanakh*) are good, but they come from the Caucasus.[5] In Russia itself they make excellent semi-hard cheeses that are not inferior to European and certainly superior to American cheeses.

In the United States there are imported cheeses, analogous to brands we know: "Gouda," just like "Kostroma"; "Cream Havarti," like our "Russian"; "Edam"—"Uglinsky"; "Fontina" —"Yaroslavsky"; "Dutch cheese"—"Dutch cheese."

So we had cheese, but no one knew what to do with it. On the morning after a party there were always dried yellow petals left on the plates: Russians don't consider cheese to be a real food, but they had to respect it for being expensive (twice as expensive as pork), so they put it out on the table for some reason. And what really shocked European visitors was that even in restaurants, cheese was served together with other appetizers, with herring and jellied tongue, for example.

Meanwhile, cheese is actually a dessert. (Pardon, we are talking banalities.) There is nothing more delicious after a good dinner than soft and semi-soft cheeses—Brie, Saint André, Roquefort, Gorgonzola—with grapes, pears, and apples. The cheese is served whole, and the fruit is sliced.

[1] Population 60,000, this town is located 70 km. southwest of Moscow in the direction of Kiev.

[2] The song is called "Lilies of the Valley." The hero of the song doesn't just not bring roses, he also does not bring tulips or lilies—but he does manage to bring the lilies of the valley.

[3] Rot-front here is a perversion of the word Roquefort.

[4] The *plavlennyi syrok*, or processed cheese square, comes in 100 gram packages and is good in a pinch if you need to have a bite with your vodka. See note to chapter 29.

[5] *Chanakh* is an Armenian cheese brined in small pots called "chans," while *suluguni* is Georgian brine cheese.

The main function of cheese is dessert. But its other culinary possibilities were also unknown to Russian cuisine: In the best case scenario, we ate grated cheese on our pasta and scrambled eggs. But a cheese schnitzel made of mozzarella, provolone, or Greek kasseri cheese is a subtle and at the same time filling dish, simpler to make than an omelet. You only need to cool the cheese: It should be iced for about two hours.

Cut a slice 1 inch thick, roll it in egg and flour, and toss into the pan with preheated oil. Just a minute on each side, and the schnitzel is ready. Add olives, herbs, lettuce. A sunny-side up egg also makes a lovely complement to cheese schnitzel.

Cheese is delicious added into cutlets. Grind a piece of cheddar cheese with the meat and other usual ingredients for a cutlet. Your proportions should be 1 part cheese to 2 parts meat. The patties will be juicy and savory, with only one drawback: They won't be tasty cold. But why eat cold cutlets? In the past, for some reason, they occupied a disproportionately large place in our diet.

Many vegetables—broccoli, cauliflower, zucchini—make elegant dishes if you bake them sprinkled with freshly grated cheese. For a sharper taste, choose cheddar, for a milder one—Swiss.

A slice of cheese will almost always improve a piece of meat cooking in the oven or in a frying pan. Little pieces of cheese, coated in egg, flour, and egg, and again in breadcrumbs, and then fried in oil make a subtle accompaniment to veal, stewed fish, or scallops. Add 1/2 cup of grated cheese atop a plate of vegetable or mushroom soup just off the stove, and you will once again become convinced of the superiority of democracy.[6]

---

[6] Russians generally eat soup in soup plates—wide, shallow bowls. See note to chapter 20.

CHAPTER 34

Veal Tenderness

The traditional Russian attitude toward veal was always more tender than carnivorous: we preferred petting a calf to eating one. That's why veal dishes are uncharacteristic in Russian cooking. If we valued this type of meat, then it was for its abundant gristle, which satisfies our national craving for a peculiar second-ratedness. Recall that treat for patriots: aspic ("For little Abraham—matzo; for little Nathan—matzo; and for Ivan-Mólodets—a piece of *kholodets*"—Vasily Aksyonov wrote quite rightly in his novel *The Burn*).[1]

But in the West, veal is king, even judging by the price. Veal is a boon companion to democratic spinelessness, and we must soften our customs and explore this food, even at the cost of material loss.

Since veal's value is in its tenderness, the chef must succeed in bringing its unique subtlety to the table. Free the meat from its bounteous skin, gristle, and tendons and then put it in a very hot pan without oil to quickly sear it. Youth always needs to be protected, and searing the flesh will protect the veal from even the most hapless cook.

Now you're half done. You can finish a few different ways. For example, you can make a soup which we might call Breath of Spring.

---

[1] Ivan-Molodets here is a hybrid of Ivan Tsarevich and the folkloric epithet *dobry molodets*, a heroic young man. We might remember Pushkin's "A tale is a lie, but it holds a hint: a lesson for young heroes" from his "Tale of the Golden Cockerel." Vasily Aksyonov's novel *The Burn* (1980), published in Italy, caused his expulsion from the Soviet Union. Called by the *New York Times* a "jazz-inspired riff," the novel explores the plight of intellectuals under Communism. For *studen* and *kholodets*, see note in chapter 38.

Western abundance muddles the seasons together. Everything is always in season here, as though we were living on the equator. But, like Gilyarovsky said, "Who eats whitefish with a March cucumber in August?"[2] Remember the seasons, and your life will be four times richer.

So, on an April morning, throw your seared veal into a pot of boiling water with a new potato, a few florets of cauliflower, celery, parsley root, and maybe a turnip and some green peas (better straight out of the pod than canned). Simmer the soup for about 30 to 40 minutes, then sprinkle heavily with dill and fresh-ground black pepper. Eat with sour cream, sherry, and guests.

Spring will enter your home, no worse than the one Tyutchev wrote about.[3]

But you can and even must try veal roast. Cover the seared meat with ground sweet pepper (the famous Hungarian paprika).[4] Don't be stingy. It's not spicy at all, so no need to worry. Pour half a cup of dry white wine into the pot, cover, and steam for a half hour over a low flame. Then add salt, cover with cream, add a little crushed garlic and give it another 5-7 minutes on the stove.

Eat this with any noodle and pickles. Veal cooked this way evokes vague Magyar associations: czardas, the Danube, 1956.[5] It's food with political undertones.

But we imagine that you have some of those super-expensive cuts of veal, which, rumor has it, are eaten by elderly Floridian women and Baryshnikov. Don't be shy. They're just people like everyone else. Beat the meat with a wooden mallet until it is semi-transparent. Next carefully bread it. That is to say, dip it in egg, dredge in flour or semolina, then in crumbs. Quickly fry it in sizzling oil. Squeeze a lemon onto the meat, sprinkle with capers, adorn with a lettuce leaf—and voilà, Wiener Schnitzel. That's what we ate in our very first days of emigration, served by sweet old ladies at Viennese taverns.

Incidentally, if you add grated cheese to the breading mixture, it will be Schnitzel Milanese, which is also somehow linked to our émigré youth.

Pavel Petrovich Petukh, treating Chichikov to dinner at his home, said about a veal roast: "I raised it on milk for two years, nursed it like my own son!"[6]

Only once you've prepared veal properly can such a statement begin to make sense.

[2] Vladimir Alekseevich Gilyarovsky (1855–1935) was an eclectic Russian author, journalist, and actor. Vail and Genis paraphrase a thought from his best-known work, *Moscow and Muscovites*, "Don't bring me pickled March whitefish with fresh cucumbers in August!" See also note to chapter 14.

[3] Fyodor Ivanovich Tyutchev (1803–73) was a poet and contemporary of (or, as Valery Bryusov claimed in 1910, alternative to) Pushkin. His poem "Spring Storm" (1828) delights in nature's thunderous return after winter's long austerity.

[4] See note on paprika in chapter 40.

[5] The Magyars were the main indigenous tribe of Hungary. The czardas is a national folk dance with a slow first movement and a wild, fast second one. The Danube is the main river in Eastern Europe, running through four national capitals, including Budapest. The Hungarian Uprising of 1956 was brutally crushed by the Soviet army.

[6] Pyotr Petrovich Petukh is a character from Nikolai Gogol's *Dead Souls*, volume two. He takes his surname from the Russian word for rooster. *Dead Souls*, Gogol's satirical portrait of the Russian countryside, features many such exaggerated characters, a number of whom are obsessed in one or another way about food. Petukh is not to be confused with Pavel Petrovich (Kirsanov), the Anglophile uncle in Ivan Turgenev's 1862 novel *Fathers and Children*. It's possible that V&G make this conflation in misidentifying Gogol's character.

CHAPTER 35

Enjoy the Steam

Steam has always had a unique, mystical meaning for the Russian people. But it's not the practical application of steam that interests them. On the contrary, it alarms and frightens them. When the Brothers Cherepanov built their famous steam engine and laid out the railroad in the 1830s, people were so cautious that they used horse traction to pull the cars along the cast-iron rails. It is notable that the Cherepanovs' steam engine never went anywhere, and horses ran along their tracks even in the twentieth century. The only well-known use for steam among the Russian people is the *banya*.[1]

No one will deny that just like the pathetic English, you can simply wash dirt off in a basin. The banya has another purpose entirely. That is to say: national exceptionalism. Throughout the course of Russian history, the steam bath that amazed the apostle Andrew has continued to astonish foreigners and grimy native intellectuals alike.[2]

---

[1] *Banya* is the Russian word for bathhouse or sauna, which can translate as the outbuilding in the countryside where people bathed on a weekly basis. Not for nothing was a book about Russian magic titled *The Bathhouse at Midnight*, in which W. F. Ryan explores magic and divination across Russian history.

---

[2] St. Andrew the Apostle is the patron saint of Russia, Ukraine, and Romania (among other nations). In the early days of Christianity, he preached in Eastern Europe and travelled as far north as Kiev and even Novgorod. He is quoted by Nestor in *the Russian Primary Chronicle* (1133): "'Wondrous to relate,' said he, 'I saw the land of the Slavs, and while I was among them, I noticed their wooden bathhouses. They warm them to extreme heat, then undress, and after anointing themselves with an acid liquid, they take young branches and lash their bodies. They actually lash themselves so violently that they barely escape alive. Then they drench themselves with cold water, and thus are revived. They think nothing of doing this every day, and though tormented by none, they actually inflict such voluntary torture upon themselves. Indeed, they make of the act not a mere washing but a veritable torment.'" (Laurentian Text, 54)

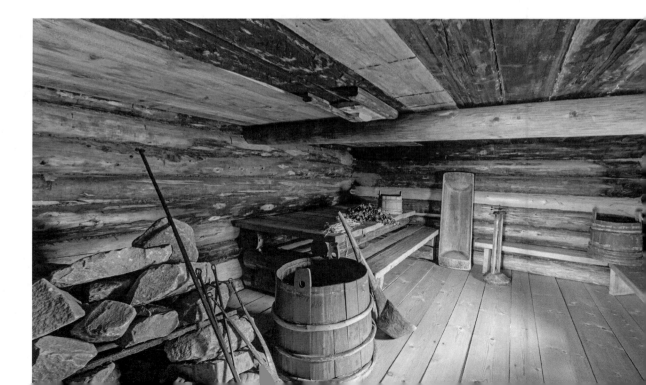

Patriots have seen the bathhouse as an uncontestable argument for the wholesome cleanliness and spiritual warmth of the Russian people. It's no accident that Andropov, that English language expert and admirer of jazz, went after banyas with a real fury.[3] And it's also no accident that a black banya—invisible from the air—was concealed under the tennis court at Alexander Isayevich Solzhenitsyn's Vermont estate.[4]

The metaphysical role of steam means you cannot take a utilitarian approach to it. That is why in Russia steam cooking suffered the same fate as the Cherepanov steam engine: utterly forgotten. The steam cooker cannot catch on in a country where the steam bath reigns. In the banya a banquet generally consists of only two items anyway: 1) beer and 2) vodka.

When we emigrated to the West, we were surprised to discover the opposite: steam baths are nowhere to be found, but steam cookers are common. This is no small consolation, especially since steaming food has an extraordinary effect, particularly when you use familiar ingredients. They will reveal themselves anew.

For example, make a fish soup in a steam cooker, and you will understand that it was worth it to emigrate. It's best to use a bamboo steamer. Failing that, a metal European one or a pot that comfortably fits a ceramic bowl will do. Place the bowl onto the grill of the steamer or on a rack at the bottom of the pot. Put finely diced onion, pieces of carrot, and a fish fillet (frozen is fine) in the bowl. Add salt, a bay leaf, and parsley root. Pour water into the lower part of the steamer or the bottom of the pot. Cover the works tightly and place it on the burner. When the water reaches a boil, reduce the flame and walk away. After about 2 hours, check that all the water hasn't boiled off, and add boiling water if necessary. After another 2 hours or so, a heavenly soup will be ready in the bowl. All of the ingredients (fish, vegetables, and broth) will be unusual and unbelievably tasty. Of course, this soup takes a long time, but it's no real trouble: the steam does everything for you.

For natural food nuts, a steam cooker is ideal. Steaming food causes the fewest nutrients to be lost. Dieters praise steam because they can cook without oils of any kind. Gourmets value steam cooking because it preserves the food's essential taste.

It's risky to assert that learning steam cooking will compensate for the absence of the steam bath, but it will add flavor to your life. That's just how it goes with nostalgic compromises.

[3] Yuri Andropov (1914–84) was head of the KGB from 1967 to 1982 and Soviet Premier from 1982 to 1984. Andropov had the idea of instituting raids on banyas during the day in order to catch people who were skipping work.

[4] The main distinction of a "black" banya is that the stove lacks a flue, and thus the soot darkens the walls. They are more prevalent in the deep countryside. Solzhenitsyn, of course, had no such hidden banya— here V&G are simply playing games.

[5] A "dietary cafeteria" was the Soviet cross between a health food outlet and a fast food joint, part of the vast public catering system.

Fish, seafood, and vegetables benefit most of all from cooking over steam. Running green beans, broccoli, or brussels sprouts through the steamer beats any submersion cooking technique for taste. After steaming vegetables, you need only add a pat of butter. For scallops, first add salt and a mixture of dried parsley, dill, and tarragon. Put it all in the steamer, and remove 8–10 minutes after the water reaches a boil.

Before steaming fish, you should generously salt it and sprinkle it with herbs, and also cover it with a layer of minced onions and carrots. Central Asian manty and dumplings are the most famous steamed meat dishes, the pride of Soviet dietary cafeterias.[5] Of course, no self-respecting person would eat steamed dumplings without a tasty sauce, which basically violates the whole idea of steaming as a healthy way to prepare food.

CHAPTER 36

Neither Fish nor Fowl

To us, the tuna was always one of the more exotic forms of seafood. Tuna was something that foreign daredevils in their white yachts caught on the open ocean using expensive, specialized fishing gear. It seems like this scene was repeated in every Western book about the romance of the good life: The tuna would rise up, their silvery scales flashing rainbow colors in the sun. We didn't even suspect that this glamorous fish belongs to the same family as the vulgar *skumbrya*, which along with the shanny and the goatfish forms Odessa's national trio.[1]

But then, in translated Western novels the *skumbrya* was called a mackerel, and you had to emigrate to find out that they were the same thing.

The tuna was also dethroned. It turns out that the shelves of every supermarket in the United States groan with cans of this food. And "tuna salad"—the house special of every greasy spoon—is made from these canned goods as well. Tuna is so abundant that the label bears the condescending name "Chicken of the Sea" (i.e., "Wet Chicken").[2] In the same way that no one can imagine a non-canned sprat, the image of tuna is connected with these little round metal tins. Many people probably think that's how tuna swim, in tidy little cylinders.

---

[1] Bullhead and striped mullet are two more names for these fish. "Shanny" and "goatfish" are more obscure names, but they lend a certain exotic flavor to the text.

---

[2] Advertising slogans rarely translate very well. If for an American "chicken of the sea" elevates tuna fish, to the Russian ear the nickname denigrated both fish and chicken.

In point of fact tuna look a lot like other big fish and can measure up to three meters long. And the secret is that the meat of tuna is a lot like meat. Even raw, the exposed face of the meat is a bloody red color, like a cut of beef or game meat. An inexperienced person could easily mistake a cooked tuna steak for beef. We'd love to encourage such pranks, but there's little humor in them. Tuna's not exactly a cheap fish, so the joke would be on us.

A tuna steak is a festive and fancy dish, which you should garnish and serve like a normal steak. The particulars of cooking it consist in how not to dry out this already fairly dry meat. That's why you need to bread your pieces of tuna carefully to keep it moist. It's best to dredge them first in flour and then in fine semolina (this is finer than breadcrumbs).[3] You should cook the steaks with a lot of onion and butter, which will basically become the sauce.

Tuna goes perfectly with vegetables. Sear the fillet (3 minutes per side). Prepare a mixture of finely diced onion, bell pepper, tomatoes, squash (zucchini), parsley, and basil. Salt, pepper, and sauté in a pan. After about 5 minutes, add a pinch of nutmeg. Cover the tuna steaks with this mixture and cook for about 15 minutes over a low flame.

It's also nice to add a half pound of fresh champignon mushrooms to this vegetable medley. They add juice and combine nicely with the taste of the tuna.

To serve, garnish with a Provençale blend of chopped spring onion, capers, and chopped olives, flavored with pepper and vinegar.

Poaching the tuna in wine doesn't really work. The thing is, the texture of tuna meat is also similar to beef, and wine toughens the flesh even more. On the contrary, you need to try to soften tuna meat, which will make it tastier and more savory. For example, you can marinate the tuna steaks in kefir for an hour or two, then bread and fry. In this way, you get an elegant dish and a sobriety measure to boot. Although this isn't the pressing issue it is at home, using kefir instead of wine will still meet with approval in conservative circles.

Just don't forget to serve the tuna with sherry or dry wine, and not white wine, as is usual with fish, but red, as with meat.

[3] Semolina is known in Russian as *mannaya krupa*, from which the beloved hot breakfast porridge *mannaya kasha* is prepared. Served with a pat of butter, this kasha ruled university cafeterias.

91

The Moveable Feast[1]

The relative prosperity of America has had its way with our waistlines. Some became more expansive, others reduced. Some of us are still savoring the carnivorous possibilities of the West, while others try to rein in their rebellious flesh with no-cal miracle tea. But on the whole, our culinary traditions turned out to be significantly stronger than all the other threads that tie us to home. The émigré might switch out *The Captain's Daughter* for *The Joy of Sex*, but no hot dog will ever replace a garlic sausage in his heart.[2]

However, the rapacious system of American fast food stands like a roadblock between the émigré and that coveted sausage.[3] Russians treat a restaurant trip as a festive occasion, while here it's a grim everyday routine. Such meals make life easier, but they castrate the soul.

Standardized cooking isn't so bad, except for the ubiquitous breading to which Americans subject everything, from fish fillets to napkins. Still, it's quite possible to survive fast food. After all, portions are large, prices are low, and there's plenty of room at the restaurant.

But true culinary ideas don't reside in restaurant kitchens. Even in the best of all restaurants (Chinese), a foreign culinary idea resides (a Chinese one). So in an attempt to master their nostalgia émigrés tend to open their own newspapers and restaurants. However, even as the lack of censors facilitates the former's success, the lack of OBKhSS is no boon to the latter.[4]

No one can make a real ukha, shchi, or *manpar* in a foreign land. You'll never come across a *kulebiaka*, *rasstegei*, or a suckling pig with kasha in an émigré restaurant.[5] Even borscht suffers from a criminally limited set of ingredients. But before you begin to throw stones at our restaurant owners, remember that they are driven by financial interests, not gastronomical ones. Let God be their judge.

No, émigrés must shoulder the sweet burden of Russian cooking at their own hearths. Only here, at home, does the enthusiast lean over the pan, clay pot, or oven fork to conjure the essence of his native land in a foreign environment. This is home cooking.

Oddly enough, you will find opponents of this wonderful phenomenon in the form of snobbism, prejudice, and spiritual laziness. Certain unhealthy elements in our midst consider home cooking to be banal. If we were to listen to the ludicrous arguments of these superfluous men, we would think that every home has only one possible menu: first, second, and third courses of, say, borscht, roasted meat, and stewed fruit.[6]

But let's hear these naysayers tell us how they cook. If, according to Heraclitus, you never step in the same river twice, then it's even more impossible to make the same borscht twice. A cafeteria cook can, with depressing regularity, concoct one and the same meal, something that never happens at home. Home cooking has an arbitrary quality to it, willfulness, even luck. In other words—inspiration. Everything here relies on nuance, shades of gray, mood— just like in the plays of Chekhov. Even a basic fried egg will melt from tenderness if you're making it for your beloved for breakfast. And that very same fried egg will turn into a dry crust if you're cooking it for a relative who's overstayed his welcome.

None of the noble arts, not even ballet or literature, offers such opportunity for fantasy and variation as cooking does. And none of the arts so disposes one toward self-expression.

2 *The Captain's Daughter*, like everything written by A. S. Pushkin, is considered a classic of Russian literature. *The Joy of Sex*, by Alex Comfort, was first published in 1972 and was very popular in America for much of the 1970s.

3 V&G rail against American fast food while retaining some fond memories for the Soviet version of this phenomenon, the cafeterias and snack bars known by the collective abbreviation *Obshchepit*, the system of public nutrition which might be translated as "social dining" or "public catering."

4 The Department Against Misappropriation of Socialist Property was the financial police force in the Soviet Union. It was (at least nominally) charged with regulation of currency, goods, and trading in accordance with Soviet economic doctrine.

5 *Manpar* is a kind of Central Asian dumpling, often served in vegetable soup, while *kulebiaka* and *rasstegai* are pastries with fish, meat, or even mushroom fillings. The kulebiaka is a covered pastry, sometimes with thin pancakes separating each layer of filling, while the rasstegai is open at the top.

6 "Superfluous men" reign in nineteenth-century Russian literature, and here they even have opinions about home cooking. They are usually talented, intelligent young men who find themselves unwilling or unable to interact meaningfully with society. Prominent examples include Pushkin's Eugene Onegin, Mikhail Lermontov's Pechorin and Turgenev's Rudin.

A meal made by a friend can say more about him than his doctor, lawyer, and psychoanalyst taken together. Food reveals a person's deepest secrets. He may read Horace in the original Latin, but when you see him smearing caviar on black bread, his carefully hidden plebeian roots are brought out into the open.[7]

Cuisine is indeed a language, a tongue with the richest possibilities. It's full of epithets and metaphors, hyperbole and litotes, metonymy and synecdoche. It's not for nothing the poet Pushkin earned his place in the memory of generations as the author of the "Pushkin-style potatoes" recipe, famed in Russian pubs (a whole potato boiled in its jacket and then baked in melted butter over coals).[8]

Can you really call a tradition banal just because it remains the same?

You can. But remember that only honest truths are banal. And the original and extravagant only blooms against the background of the ordinary.

However, good home cooking can maintain its patriarchal and conservative nature without shying away from the exotic. A shrewd cook can combine an Italian appetizer of raw oysters with Romanian spinach and feta soup and a Russian roast in a clay pot. All that's needed is a sense of harmony: a happy combination of native and foreign, just like Pushkin himself.[9]

Cuisine can really only exist in a dialectical synthesis: *svoi* and *chuzhoi*,[10] intellectual and emotional, old and new. In this sense, cuisine operates on the level of immortal categories. After all, a person has to eat every day....

[7] Quintus Horatius Flaccus (65–68 BCE), was among the great Latin lyricists. V&G's use of him as an example (rather than Ovid or Virgil) is interesting, since Horace himself "carefully hid" his roots as the son of a freed slave. More important in the context is that one should *never* eat caviar on black bread, only on fresh white bread, preferably *kalach*.

[8] Funny, given Pushkin's status as the most important writer and poet of the nineteenth century, that he be associated with baked potatoes. But this is in the tradition of Pushkin as a household name: When Soviet children didn't want to help out around the home, their parents would sometimes say "Who's going to take care of [the trash, the dishes, the mess, etc.], Pushkin?"

[9] Pushkin, a Russian aristocrat by birth, was descended from a favored adopted African child of Peter the Great, and thus occupies a dual identity of both native and foreign: Russian, but with African blood mixed in. Dostoevsky claimed, in a speech commemorating the poet's death, that Pushkin was the clarion voice of the Russian people, yet possessed a "universal sympathy," which granted him "the capacity of fully identifying himself with an alien nationality." In this he achieved what Dostoevsky considered to be the goal of the Russian spirit: the leadership of a pan-humanity (*vsechelovechestvo*).

[10] The binary of *svoi* and *chuzhoi*, "ours" and something "foreign," dominates Russian cultural understanding.

CHAPTER 38

The Non-False Non-Hare

95

When Solzhenitsyn came out with his famous appeal to "live not by lies," he may not have understood with complete clarity just how much the lie had found its way into every pore of Soviet society, eroding the nation's organism at its very foundation.[1]

Flagrant examples of deception occur even in such a pivotal sphere of human activity as food. The disgusting swill called "meatless borscht" hides beneath a vague code, "borscht b/m." "Meat of the fourth sort" means bones worn down by time, a decoction of which would deter even ill-bred mutts. A thick stew of hooves and gelatin is called *studen* and costs 36 kopeks per kilogram.[2] In the common cafeteria expression "natural ground beef," only the word "ground" was true.

All these and hundreds of similar facts are some of the regime's greatest crimes. But official lies reached the peak of hypocrisy and treachery in the name "false hare."

What does this phrase really mean? There's a hint of game meat here, and a simultaneous denial that implies something even better. However, we all recall that in the "false hare" everything was fake: from the name to its attribution to the glorious cohort of meat products.

In emigration, we can finally exercise Solzhenitsyn's message in deed. Here anyone can bravely call the Politburo a bloody gang of executioners, America his welcoming second homeland, and himself a Jew, a dissident, and an author without having to hide.

It's time to expose the pseudonym "false hare." In civilized countries, they call it meat terrine.[3] In America there is something that resembles it (meatloaf), but it's not quite the same thing. Real meat terrine is a universal dish. It can be a main course, a cold zakuska, or an essential ingredient of an open-faced sandwich.

---

[1] Alexander Solzhenitsyn's 1974 essay, "Live Not By Lies," advocates for a dedication to truth as both the most effective and the easiest form of resistance to the Soviet oppression apparatus. Solzhenitsyn was arrested the day the essay is dated and was immediately exiled to Western Europe.

---

[2] On *borscht b/m,* see *Introduction* (*Expressions of the Soul*) above. *Studen*, also called *kholodets*, is known as aspic in the West. A mainstay of the Russian diet, it is a savory gelatin *zakuska* which functions as both appetizer and drinking snack.

---

[3] The Russian term here is "meat pudding," which evokes Dickensian London.

Fry a large, finely diced onion and a little bit of celery (about a tablespoon) in some oil. Allow the onion to reach a golden hue. In a large bowl mix 1/2 pound of ground beef, the fried onion, 1/2 cup of oatmeal, 1/2 cup of ketchup, and 1/2 cup of milk or water. Add seasonings: one tablespoon of dried parsley, a pinch of cumin, and—this is essential—about a tablespoon of dried marjoram. Add salt and pepper to taste. Put half of this mixture into an oblong mold, thick enough that the whole loaf will reach 8–10 centimeters in height. Then add your filling, and on top—the other half of the mixture. Put it in the oven for 40–50 minutes at 350–375 degrees.

The most interesting and creative part of making a terrine is choosing the filling. It will not do to stifle your imagination on this. You just have to remember that the terrine will be carved into thick slices when it's ready, so you need to stuff it with a filling that will look attractive and not fall out. Sausages and long strips of bacon can be set end-to-end. Cut hard-boiled eggs in half lengthwise. Choose average-sized pickles and lay them whole along the length of the terrine. Fried or boiled mushrooms don't need to be cut either. Almost anything can make a good filling, such as fried chicken liver, smoked cheese, or baked eggplant.

A prepared terrine will keep in the refrigerator, and you can reheat slices on a low flame and serve with any garnish in a rich sauce: mushroom, sour cream and mustard, or sour cream and horseradish. You can take sandwiches of terrine with a lettuce leaf to work or on a picnic. In the universal dish you have prepared, there's no hare, but there's nothing false, either. Just one more step on the path to truth.

Sober
Drunkenness

The exquisite culinary technique of introducing alcohol to a dish is one that Russian tradition has developed to a subtle art. Usually it is introduced in faceted glasses, but it's also possible to introduce it in your most elegant stemware.[1]

It's curious that in contrast to Italian or French cuisine, Russian cuisine permits the mixing of alcohol with almost any food. With processed cheese, for example.[2] Who are we to argue? We would never raise a hand to alter native culinary traditions. And yet let us note that sometimes, as an exception, it's possible to use alcohol in the process of preparing food and not only while consuming it.

But then, one does not prevent the other. Especially if you keep in mind that when you heat them up, spirits disappear without a trace, which seems like such a shame.

As everyone knows, alcohol has strange but pleasant qualities. In cuisine, as in life in general, it is irreplaceable. Let's say you are making ukha. And sooner or later everyone does. If a clever chef manages to obtain sturgeon for the ukha, then he will pour a generous glass of dry champagne into the pot before he turns off the gas. Sturgeon love luxury.

Ukha made from a simpler fish can get by very well with vodka; 50 grams per pot will add a certain pungency to the dish and will give the fish strength and a white color.

Alcohol in the kitchen is good in that it adds piquancy to the most everyday dish. For example, chicken. Take some chicken breasts, cut them in half, gently tenderize them, add salt and red and black pepper, roll in egg and bread crumbs, and then quickly (one minute per side) fry them in heated oil. Then add a jigger of dry sherry to the frying pan and throw in a handful of capers. Voilà! Elegant, quick, cheap, and unusual.

Despite the widespread delusion, beer is good with more than just crab. Let us prove it. Cut a beef fillet into pieces about the size of a woman's palm. (There is a cannibalistic nostalgia in culinary terminology: "bloody," "a finger's width.") Tenderize the meat, salt and pepper it and lightly fry on a dry pan until a crust is formed.

Put the meat into a pot, and in the remaining juices sauté some onion and carrot. Cover the pieces of meat with the vegetables and some pieces of black bread smeared liberally with mustard. Then pour in a can of any light beer, add caraway seeds and a bay leaf, cover, and stew for 2 hours. At the very end add 1 tablespoon of sugar and 1 of vinegar.

Alcohol is also used for making Americans' favorite dessert—baked Alaska. This is so simple that it's embarrassing to write it down. The only trick to making this dish is to time the electricity properly. Pour any brandy over any ice cream. Then touch a match to the "Alaska" and—Attention!—turn out the lights. This is what they do at White House state dinners.

[1] Faceted glassware has existed in Russia since the time of Peter the Great. It is more solid than a normal drinking glass, making it useful for drinking parties and travel, and is the most common type of glass to be used when drinking tea. The Soviet faceted glass was designed by Vera Mukhina, the famous sculptor of the Worker and Peasant statue at Moscow's *VDNKh* that also features in Mosfilm opening credits.

[2] See note to chapter 33 on the *plavlennyi syrok*.

But we know a better dessert. We brought this secret from Italy, where the hospitable Italians treated us to milk with Amaretto liqueur (3/4 of a glass of milk to 1/4 liqueur). An unaccustomed combination for the Russian palate, but strikingly delicious. Men, women, and growing children love it, since it reminds them of the halcyon days of émigré transit.

As the reader can see, the use of alcohol in matters culinary knows no bounds. Thus a good chef who likes to experiment should always keep a complete collection of bottles in the kitchen—vodka, brandy, champagne, white and red dry wines, sherry, madeira, liqueurs. The main difficulty is in using this wealth in a cultured way—not drinking it all at once, but adding a little bit at a time to whatever dish your taste buds and imagination prompt you.

Many people, even among our fellow countrymen, are infected with the silliest prejudice. They believe that soup is an insignificant intermezzo between appetizer and entrée. This is not merely cheap snobbery acquired at bad restaurants. It is an example of that pure barbarity with which truly enlightened people have always had to struggle.

Soup is the pinnacle of the culinary arts in which a new unity is achieved via a complex synthesis of various foods. To sufficiently appreciate the virtues of soup, you should try to create a meal consisting of only one dish—soup. Of course, the delicious but ordinary chicken bouillon will not do. Such a meal requires beauty, and loftiness, and even ritual. The best of these qualities can be found in a bouillabaisse, which—in the manner of Provence—we consider to be the king of all soups.

Despite its high-flown title, bouillabaisse, like all authentic cultural treasures, comes from the people. The fishermen of southern France made it from the unsold leavings of their catch.

Which is why, by the way, lobster is foreign to bouillabaisse. American chefs only add it to justify their astronomical prices. But luxury cannot replace art, and the long recipe for bouillabaisse requires a real artist to manage it properly.

CHAPTER 40

The First Is Also the Last[1]

First of all, make a stock from all kinds of small fish, plus onion, carrot, bay leaf, and pepper. Strain after simmering for 1/2 hour. Then sweat finely chopped onion and garlic (about five cloves) in olive oil in a large soup pot for 2 to 3 minutes. When the mixture begins to smell like Provence, pour the stock into the pot along with a cup of dry white wine and a can of tomatoes with their juice (first press the tomatoes against the side of the can with a fork). Now it's time to think about the spices by adding a so-called "bouquet garni" to the pot. This consists of

---

[1] A possible biblical allusion to Matthew 20:16, "So the last will be first and the first will be last." But more importantly, the first course in a Russian meal is soup, and the second is the entrée, which means that in brief people say things like: "What are we having for first? for second?"

a bay leaf, some chopped parsley, orange zest, and a pinch of basil, plus (without fail!) 1/2 cup of saffron-infused water.

While the base for the bouillabaisse simmers (about 15 minutes), you can get to work on the mussels. They must be carefully washed, put into a frying pan, and warmed until the shells begin to open and give off some juice.

The rest depends on your creativity and your stinginess. Any fish goes into bouillabaisse, and the more varied the types, the tastier. Just remember that a firm fish, like cod, should be put in five minutes earlier than a tender fish like halibut. It's best to use fillets, though Provence fishermen don't bother themselves with cleaning the fish.

Cook the bouillabaisse with the fish for no more than 15 to 20 minutes; 5 minutes before it is done, add the prepared mussels and—if you don't mind the cost—a dozen raw, shelled shrimp.

However, you're not done yet. Bouillabaisse is unthinkable without a "rouille" sauce. The simplest recipe (actually we don't even know a complicated one) is to take mayonnaise (the mild European kind is better) and mix it with olive oil, paprika, and a huge amount of crushed garlic.[2] And you need to mix it. Long and hard.

But you're still not done. It's not enough to prepare a bouillabaisse; you need to know how to eat it properly. Pour the soup into a pre-warmed soup tureen. Give napkins out to your hungry guests (and don't invite the other kind!), who should wrap themselves as if they were at the barbershop. Place several small dishes on the table, one each for the sauce, white bread croutons, and garlic cloves. A clever guest will grate the garlic on the harsh dried surface of the crouton, spread some sauce on it and eat with the soup, rolling his eyes back in his head with delight.

Bouillabaisse should be eaten slowly and in great quantities—about five bowls of it. There's no need to drink anything with it. But in the middle of the feast you can make a *trou Normand*. That is, drink a large shot of Calvados and sit quietly for five minutes or so. Superstitious French people believe that such an operation increases the size of the stomach.

After a meal like this you will continue to taste garlic in your mouth for a day. But in this culinary hangover, as with a regular one, there is a certain languid charm known only to gluttons and drunks.

Of course, bouillabaisse has nothing whatsoever to do with "Russian cuisine." But then, it is directly connected to "exile." You would never have been able to try a dish like this at home.[3]

[2] An English cookbook might recommend red pepper flakes. Perhaps the only source of this flavoring in the Soviet Union was Hungary, with its famous metal spice boxes of paprika.

[3] Here Vail and Genis speak directly to their Russian émigré audience. Why not capitalize on the experience of that inadvertent European sojourn on the way to the United States and tweak the Russian palate?

Understandably, national cuisines differ from each other. But it's not always easy to determine clearly just how. It's all well and good when the difference is obvious: the Eskimo enjoys cold slices of raw polar explorer, and the bushman licks his chops over giraffe wings. Some find wine inviting, others invite friends to dine. Some use chopsticks at mealtime, others use mealtime for politics. Some put food on the table, others put it on their expense account.

But from a culinary point of view, it is often the fundamental technology of cooking (boiling, frying, stewing) that is specific to a nation's cuisine, or sometimes the basic material (meat, fish, grain), or perhaps the primary lubricant. European traditions are fairly clearly divided according to that last attribute. In developed cuisines, various ingredients can be used to soften up the food—to temper spiciness, to alleviate dryness, to add juiciness—but one is always dominant. For the French it's butter, for Italians and Spaniards it's olive oil, for Germans and Ukrainians it's fatback (pork fat), for Romanians and Moldovans—sunflower oil. In Russian cuisine, the primary lubricant is sour cream.

Sour cream gets added to all the most famous and delicious Russian soups (apart from ukha): shchi, solyanka, rassolnik, okroshka, and botvinya.[1]

Even in the most recent period of Russian history, given the desperate deprivation of the communal dining menu, many people breakfasted in cafeterias on half a glass of sour cream with a piece of bread—these were food products that could be relied on.[2] And how many inspired lines have been written by Russian authors about hazel grouses and quail in sour cream, or about fried smelts in sour cream, both "prime smellers"![3]

By the way, about hazel grouse and smelt. Fowl and fish really do go well with sour cream, but in this case "to fry" means to heat in a covered pot. In a frying pan sour cream will burn and acquire a bitter taste. So preparing fish or fowl in this manner is more like poaching in a sauce. First the meat should be seared—ten minutes for fowl, two minutes per side for fish, then pour sour cream over it and poach.

CHAPTER 41

The Meaning of Sour Cream

But everything is tastier if sour cream isn't the only ingredient. The most elementary additions will turn it into various sauces. A tablespoon of horseradish per cup of sour cream makes a sauce for fish or boiled meat. A tablespoon of mustard—for fried meat or chicken. Two tablespoons of finely diced pickled cucumbers (you can use cornichons) or a tablespoon of capers—for boiled fish or shrimp. Dried herbs, such as basil, marjoram, or mint, can be added to sour cream in very small quantities a minute before turning off the heat. Any of these additions or a considered combination of them will create a new dish.

An amalgamation of sour cream and mushrooms—fried or in soup—is quite common. But sour cream goes just as well with vegetables. Boil cauliflower, broccoli, or zucchini, flavoring with greens and herbs, then remove them from the liquid, grind them up (in a food processor, or dice finely), return to the liquid along with a cup of sour cream and a pinch of nutmeg and you'll have a delicious vegetarian soup.

Sour cream with paprika gives meat or fowl a Hungarian flavor as stimulating as a *czardas*.[4] Brown pieces of beef or chicken with onion, transfer to a pot, add a pinch of caraway, cayenne pepper, 2 or 3 slices of bell pepper and 2 tablespoons of paprika. Add salt [to taste]. After stewing over a low flame for 1 hour, add 3 minced cloves of garlic and 2 cups of sour cream. In five minutes you will have a delicacy that even János Kádár won't eat (he has an ulcer).[5]

But, like the imperial adventurers of old, we have accidentally wandered into neighboring foreign lands. It's of course possible to go further, for example, to recall an Alsatian omelet in which you add a tablespoon of sour cream to the usual egg and milk mixture—the omelet will not be particularly airy, but it will be filling and flavorful.

Coming back to our homeland, we again are struck by the wide use of sour cream in all areas of cooking—in appetizers, soups, entrees, desserts. In order to fully appreciate the Russian lubricant, we make a sour cream and cabbage *karavai*—a unique dish which really amazes foreigners.[6]

Place cabbage leaves on the bottom of a large, deep frying pan with some melted butter, layering each leaf with sour cream and pressing down. Do this for 6 or 7 layers, slather the entire construction with sour cream, sprinkle with bread crumbs and place in the oven for 1/2 hour. When you take it out, cut it like a pie, and you will come to understand the superiority of our national lubricant over the olive oil of the Italians, the fatback of the Germans, and so on—see above.

---

[1] *Okroshka* is a cold soup made up of raw vegetables and cooked meat, diced and mixed with kvass just before serving with sour cream. For more on *ukha*, see chapter 20, *shchi*, chapter 3, *solyanka*, chapter 6, *rassolnik*, chapter 29, and *botvinya*, chapter 17.

[2] See note to chapter 37 on Soviet cafeterias.

[3] From Anton Chekhov's "The Siren" (1887), in which the court secretary Zhilin's passionate ramblings about food drive his captive audience mad with appetite.

[4] The *czardas* is a traditional Hungarian folk dance, but the word actually derives from the old Hungarian term for tavern.

[5] János Kádár was General Secretary of the Hungarian Communist Party from 1956 to 1988.

[6] The *karavai* or *korovai* is a festive loaf with ancient, agrarian connotations in Russian culture.

103

CHAPTER 42

Breadslicers at Work

ИЗДЕЛИЯ ИЗ ТЕСТА

ДРОЖЖЕВОЕ ТЕСТО

Дрожжевое, или, как его иначе называют, кислое тесто используют для выпечки разнообразных изделий: пирожков, пирогов, кулебяк, булочек, ватрушек, пончиков и т. п.

Дрожжи, положенные при замесе теста, сбраживают содержащиеся в муке сахаристые вещества, разлагая их на углекислый газ и спирт. Углекислый газ, образующийся в тесте в виде пузырьков, поднимает тесто и разрыхляет его.

Для приготовления теста расходуется дрожжей от 20 до 50 г на каждый килограмм муки. Чем больше положено в тесто сдобы (масла, яиц, сахара), тем больше надо брать и дрожжей. Дрожжи должны быть свежие, мягкие, с приятным спиртным запахом.

При замесе теста дрожжи разводят теплой водой или теплым молоком. Наиболее благоприятная температура для развития дрожжей 25—30°. Холодная вода или хо-

Nothing is worse than American bread. The difference between the two superpowers becomes clearest of all in how they relate to this food. We loved it. Wise Soviet political bureaucrats pronounced: "Bread is the head of it all," as they bought American grain.[1] Americans were happy to share, because here bread is despised.

Only hatred could explain how Americans manage to bake the cottony abomination which the savages, in their madness, accept as bread. "But we have no problem giving up baked goods," locals insist. Sure, it's easy to say no to baked goods like these, but then again, it is also a simple matter to kill a man.

The Russian (please note) scientist Timiryazev said that a hunk of good baked bread is the greatest accomplishment of the human intellect. That's what we're talking about. Not the airplane, not the Mona Lisa, but a plain loaf of bread. Only, where can we get our hands on this loaf? Thank the Lord, we are not alone in our bread nostalgia. When they arrive in America, all immigrants start with a bakery. Wherever entrepreneurial bakers of the third wave have yet to arrive, there are certainly German, Ukrainian, and Baltic shops selling rye goods.

However, those porous American loaves do serve a purpose. They make good toast. Regardless of how easy this dish is, it still requires some culinary education. Beat two eggs with a splash of milk, add salt, pepper, and dried parsley, and lay four pieces of ordinary packaged white bread in the mixture. Wait until the liquid has completely soaked into the soft bread, then fry in butter until it is a nice golden color. The resulting toast/scrambled egg hybrid is called French toast, and it makes a complete breakfast all by itself.

It's just as easy to prepare the fancy-sounding dish *consommé avec diables*. A consommé is any clear broth, and here's how to make the diables—"devilish" croutons. Cut the white bread into shapes (squares, diamonds, stars of David) and smear with a mixture of butter, shredded cheese, egg, and tomatoes. Then bake it in the oven, place it in a bowl, and pour the broth over it.

Bread is also good as a shortcut to making dessert. Who in our time bothers with dough? To be honest, nobody. But anyone who can read our book can make, say, carrot cake. Soak the white bread, crusts removed, in milk. Mix the resulting, sticky batter with shredded carrot, and add beaten eggs, sugar, and a pinch of salt. Mix until it becomes a uniform mass (you can use a mixer). Put the casserole in a greased pan sprinkled with breadcrumbs, and bake it in the oven for half an hour. Then serve it with whipped cream, jelly, or just sour cream.

But in order to appreciate the indispensability of bread in the Russian kitchen, you must prepare real Jewish sweet-and-sour. Even the worst anti-Semites cannot resist this dish, which, along with stuffed pike and goose cracknels, forms the glorious triumvirate of Jewish gems. It is not for us half-bloods to write about it, but if we make a mistake, our comrades can correct us.

[1] The Russian word for grain, *khleb*, also means bread. This linguistic efficiency helped make agricultural yields feel immediately significant to city dwellers who could not help but know the connection between grain production and their bakery shelves.

Trim the fat from some beef (a piece of about 3 pounds). Heat the fat in a pan, remove the cracklings, if you wish, and add the meat after cutting it into large chunks. A little later, when the meat has browned, add a lot of onions, and then pour hot water over it to cover. Now, you need to reduce the heat, cover the pot, and leave the meat to set for about 2 hours. You should get to work on the most important component—the sauce.

For this, only black bread will do—no compromises. Cut the crust off a piece of bread weighing about 300 grams and soak it in cold water. When the bread breaks down into mush, add salt, 2 tablespoons of sugar, and 1 teaspoon of citric acid. Exact measurements for this dish are impossible—it is all about personal taste and discretion. The main thing is that the sauce be sweet and sour; the nuances are a personal matter.

When the meat is almost ready, mix it with the sauce and simmer another 20 minutes. You have to eat the sweet-and-sour in a patriarchal manner, that is to say with a bunch of family members, all rolling your eyes back in your heads and licking your fingers.

A Russian proverb says, "If there is bread and kvass, we have all we need." For us [émigrés] it's precisely the bread and kvass that are the problem, but we will persevere. We knew what we were getting ourselves into.

CHAPTER 43

The West is Wind, The East is Ecstasy [1]

---

[1] Perversely—or at least that's how it feels to the translators—Vail and Genis wrote the forty-third chapter in verse. We have done our best to maintain the rhythm and a sense of the rhymes.

As we float on the current of fate to its ends,
We have changed on the way our addresses and names,
Sights and smells, sounds and signs, and the voices of friends,
All sensations and tastes, all things worth our acclaim …

BBC radio failed to give us a clue
That the New World would fight us, alone and befuddled,
Even cleaners outrank us, we're last in the queue,
We expect a hello, but get nothing but trouble.

In the stores food is measured in meaningless pounds:
Good forshmak requires how many herrings, d'you think?
They declare their tomatoes can grow above ground,
Lacking sturgeon, they offer us perch, the rat finks!

What's a foot? What's a yard? We are lost without meters.
We are sweaty from Fahrenheit: what could it mean?
To the liquor store's quarts we prefer our half-liters
For the quart double-quick speeds on drunk apogee.

For zakuska we struggle to find a syrok;
And blood sausage. And pink-as-a-rat radish too.
We require kholodets, that gelatinous rock.
Or at least warty pickles: in a pinch, they will do.

If we found us some moonshine we might start to cry,
Grab our friend by the sleeve, ask: "Remember, old man?"
How we drank bathtub gin, straight no chaser, like lye
For as long as we managed to keep glass in hand.

Young and fresh we were then, just as crisp as a radish,
Our troubles burnt off when we made our shashlik,
And we learned where to find all the truths we would cherish:
At the bottom of glasses of wine domestique.

Not for nothing did we go to battle with customs,
Beat the charges against us OVIR had unfurled.[2]
Our treasure we hid in the seams of our garments;
To Vienna, then Rome, 'cross the Ocean … the world!

In Elysian fields of fresh baby spinach
Flocks of turkeys are resting on cowberry jam,
Having tied themselves helpless with lengths of coarse twine,
on the synagogue's table, by grace of Hashem.

[2] OVIR was the Soviet Department of Visas and Registrations.

We have watched as those glistening lobsters, once black,
Turned to red like a girl in the hands of a cad;
We've seen prawns and mustachioed crayfish in steam;
And we've met with the "monk" fish, his countenance sad.

Now we've learned to decipher the real in mirage,
And find novelty plain and the diva's voice staid.
We accept Belgian endive, both noble and wan,
And asparagus, gothic and pearly, now plain.

Just imagine the wonders we've witnessed since then:
Périgord's soft aroma of foie gras it seems,
And the kindness of pigs, how politely they bend,
To procure for us truffles to rival our dreams.

The shell of the oyster swings open to beckon
Into bottomless bliss, like the depths of canyons.
And the pantry door, too, will reveal in a second
Secret treasures of lands ruled by Dom Perignon.

But the past is still more than ruins in our eyes.
All confusion,[3] we cherish the quaint dance of time:
We remember the fairy-like taste of good sturgeon
And have finally learned when to add cardamom.

We honor as holy those lard-fried potatoes,
If our lunches did not taste of shchi, we'd rebel.
We washed down lamb cutlets, so tender and fatty,
with glass after glass of that wine from Moselle.

While our bellies were savoring chic artichokes,
In the breaking of bread we smelled mem'ries and fables,
And avoiding effects of that dread culture shock,
We sat both cultures down at one unified table.

We have rescued détente from its emptiest meaning,
From the snarling and chains of political scheming.
We gave flesh to the notion through simply comingling
With two utterly different conceptions of cooking.

We await a parade that will comfort the heart,
The omnipotent chef offering cold ananas,
With some white avocado and steak from Kharkov,
Boston Red borscht and Astrakhan bananas.[4]

[1] "All is confusion" evokes the second paragraph of Leo Tolstoy's novel *Anna Karenina*: "All was confusion in the Oblonsky household."

[2] *Papirovka*, or white filling (*belyi naliv*), is a strain of cold-resistant apples in Russia. Here Vail and Genis may have in mind cold-resistant avocados, as impossible as bananas in Astrakhan (a city on the Volga), beef from the industrial city of Kharkov, and borscht from America. But of course the *ananas*, or pineapple, also features in Pushkin's famous description of exotic foods in *Eugene Onegin*.

Dear Reader!

Allow us to remove our aprons and toques and raise a ceremonial toast.

We have wearied the reader with our recipes. We have urged him to cast off his work duties, his sports, and his stamp collecting so that he might spend precious hours at the stove without distraction. We have begged the reader to cook. We have conjured him through shchi and ukha not to lose touch with his national roots. We have lifted his spirits with bouillabaisse and kharcho. We have implored him not to get caught in the trap of McDonald's and Burger King. On our knees, we have begged him not to neglect seasoning, not to brew weak tea, and not to serve fish without Sauce Provençal.

We have sometimes fallen into a polemical pathos, accusing the reader of spiritual laziness and undue loyalty to his diet. We have sometimes exposed the old men of the Kremlin for perverting the idea of rassolnik, soup with pickle juice. We have sometimes come down harshly on Americans, who are ossified by their materialism and have not perceived the meaning of cutlets.

We saw it as our literary-culinary duty to instill kind feelings toward good cooking in our bewildered émigré community. We wanted to soften the bitterness of exile with the sweetness of an apple Charlotte.

We have tested each dish presented to the reader on ourselves and our loved ones. We bid adieu with a sense of having completed our task, repeating once again the mantra of Venedikt Erofeev, "Each person has but one life, and it's necessary to live without making mistakes in recipes."

We have shared everything we know and everything we are capable of with the reader. We hope that now he will proceed to the summits of culinary wisdom without our help. At those heights gleam prizes we have not described, like pierogis with saffron milk-cap mushrooms (*rizhiki*), kholodets, chicken pie, kasha à la Guriev, heavenly

CHAPTER 44

A Toast to Gluttons[1]

---

[1] According to Russian toasting customs, toasts early in the evening tend to be more generic, while later toasts (once there is a shared level of trust, or at least drunkenness) are closer to speeches.

gefilte fish and many more, which even our wise men cannot dream up.[2] And maybe one day we will meet our reader again at the table, where he will serve these treasures.

But for the moment, we raise this toast to the humble laborer of the frying pan, to the sage of the ladle, to the pioneer of edible horizons. We drink to connoisseurs of food, to those who transform a physiological need into high art. We raise our glasses! But to avoid the banality of sloshing vodka about, allow us to offer one last recipe. Now then: holiday punch.

[2] Interestingly, almost all of these recipes turn up in Anya von Bremzen's history of Russian cuisine in the twentieth century, *Mastering the Art of Soviet Cooking.* Perhaps not a coincidence?

Take a fancy soup tureen and line the bottom with any dried fruit. Dried bananas, pineapple, apples, and apricots work, but not raisins. They are too small, and that can get annoying. Now pour 1 glass of good cognac into the tureen (and is there any better cognac than Armenian?), along with 1 glass of moderately priced rum.

Next, mull some wine in a saucepan. That is, bring 1.5 liters of any dry red wine to a boil and mix it with 2 glasses of very strong tea. Add 1/2 cup of sugar (or more), 3 or 4 cloves, 1/2 teaspoon of cinnamon, a pinch of vanilla and nutmeg, and an allspice berry or two. Don't let the mulled wine come to a boil. Remove from the flame and pour it into the soup tureen.

Now for the most colorful part of the ritual of punch preparation. Cover the bowl with some kind of screen (a metal colander, for example). Sprinkle 1/2 pound of sugar cubes onto the grate, pour rum over it, turn off all the lights, and set it on fire. While the sugar burns with a blue flame and drains into the punch, you can sing songs or simply foster a festive spirit within yourself.

Ladle the punch into teacups when it is ready, making sure that there is a little dried fruit in the bottom of each cup.

So we can complete our toast with a clear conscience. To gourmets, belly-slaves, and gluttons. To the flourishing of Russian cooking in exile!

Interview with Alexander Genis

1) **How and why did you write *Russian Cuisine in Exile*? All kinds of anecdotes and stories are welcome here: Where did you get the idea, how did you actually write (separately, together, in parallel fashion, at the table or walking in a park, and so on).**
First-wave émigrés had a popular saying: "We are not in exile, we are on a mission." That's why we particularly liked the heading Ksana Blank (Dovlatov's half-sister) thought up for us: "Russian Cuisine in Exile." The title belongs to her. We were trying to reduce the pathos that reigned in the Russian community abroad. In our struggle with the "savage seriousness" (in Aksyonov's words) of émigré rhetoric, we crafted our culinary columns to be both parodic and practical. Every dish was tested at literary dinners to which we treated virtually every writer of the third wave. Except—it goes without saying—Solzhenitsyn, who really did believe he was on a mission. We cooked our most unusual dinner for Brodsky. We stole all the dishes from Martialis (we wrote the menu in Latin, with epigrams). But he did not come—that evening he had open-heart surgery.

We always wrote separately, but we decided not to tell anyone who wrote what.

2) **How did you first publish the text, in newspapers or as a book? What publisher did you use in the beginning and to whom did they market the book?**
Our columns were printed in the weekly newspaper *Panorama*, which was published in Los Angeles. The editors collected them and published an attractive little book in 1987 with a fabulous cover created by our friend Vagrich Bakhchanyan. In the last days of the Soviet Union the book was republished (extremely badly) with a run of 20,000 copies. They sold out in one day. Since then our opus has been published again and again for the last thirty years; I've even lost track of the editions. It has also been translated, among other places in France (which is flattering) and in Japan (which is surprising).

3) **For whom did you write? That is, how did you imagine your reader?**
We wrote for people like ourselves. In the emigration there weren't many readers, we knew them all by sight. Well, almost all of them.

4) **What did your friends, your relatives, your colleagues say to you about the project as it proceeded?**
Our wives were ecstatic: finally we had found a way to combine the useful with the agreeable, and to save them from cooking.[1] Lev Loseff, the poet and professor at Dartmouth College, wrote an extensive introduction to the first edition. Dovlatov, who had no interest in culinary matters whatsoever, thought and wrote that this book could serve as a portrait of our generation.[2] I still am not sure I understand what he meant.

[1] A favorite Russian idiom which comes from the Latin. "He who joins the useful with the agreeable wins every vote, by delighting and at the same time instructing the reader." Horace, *Ars Poetica*.

[2] Dovlatov was hearkening back here to Mikhail Lermontov's 1841 novel *A Hero of our Time*, which according to the frame narrator was to serve as a portrait of his generation. The meaning of that statement, too, remains somewhat ambiguous in the novel.

5) **Did you compare your project to any other book?**
We weren't aware of any other such books, but our culinary erudition was bolstered by the marvelous books of William Pokhlebkin, that great expert, historian, and practitioner of cooking. He endorsed our project, by the way, a fact we were always proud of.

6) **How do you look on your book today?**
Like Conan Doyle on Sherlock Holmes. The Holmes stories completely eclipsed all the other writings of the author.

7) **What is your reaction to the fame and popularity of your book in Russia today? To the desire to translate it into other languages?**
You don't argue with success.

Alexander Genis

ПЕТР ВАЙЛЬ И АЛЕКСАНДР ГЕНИС
ЭМИГРИРОВАЛИ ИЗ РИГИ В НЬЮ-ЙОРК В 1977 ГОДУ
АВТОРЫ КНИГ «СОВРЕМЕННАЯ РУССКАЯ ПРОЗА» (1982),
«ПОТЕРЯННЫЙ РАЙ» (1983)

Further Reading
(in English or English Translation)

Bezmozgis, David. *The Free World* (New York: Macmillan, 2011).

Bloch, Sydney, and Peter Reddaway. *Russia's Political Hospitals: The Abuse of Psychiatry in the Soviet Union* (London: Victor Gollanz, 1977).

Chekhov, Anton. "The Siren" (1887), in *The Portable Chekhov*, edited by Avrahm Yarmolinsky, 90–97 (New York: Viking Penguin, 1975).

Crewe, Quentin. *The International Pocket Food Guide* (New York: Simon and Schuster, 1980).

Dovlatov, Sergei. *The Suitcase* (1986), translated by Antonina Bouis (Berkeley: Counterpoint, 2011).

Erofeev, Venedikt. *Moscow to the End of the Line* (1969), translated by H. William Tjalsma (Evanston: Northwestern UP, 1992).

Gessen, Masha. *Where the Jews Aren't: The Sad and Absurd Story of Birobidzhan, Russia's Jewish Autonomous Region* (New York: Nextbook, Schocken, 2016).

Gilyarovsky, Vladimir. *Moscow and Muscovites* (1926), translated by Brendan Kiernan (Montpelier, VT: Russian Information Services, 2013).

Glad, John. *Russia Abroad: Writers, History, Politics* (Hermitage and Birchbark Press, 1999).

Irina Glushchenko, *Obshchepit: Mikoyan and Soviet Cuisine* (Moscow: Vysshaia shkola ekonomiki, 2010).

Molokhovets, Elena. *A Gift to Young Housewives* (1861), translated by Joyce Toomre as *Classic Russian Cooking: Elena Molokhovets' A Gift to Young Housewives* (Bloomington: Indiana UP, 1992).

Nabokov, Vladimir. *Speak, Memory: An Autobiography Revisited* (New York: Vintage International, 1967).

Pushkin, Alexander. *Eugene Onegin* (1831), translated by James Falen (Oxford: Oxford UP, 2009).

_____. *Ruslan and Ludmilla: A Novel in Verse*, translated by Nancy Dargel (New York: Bergh, 1994).

Ries, Nancy. "Potato Ontology: Surviving Post-Socialism in Russia," *Cultural Anthropology* 24, no. 2 (2009): 181–212.

Ryan, W. F. *The Bathhouse at Midnight* (University Park: Penn State UP, 1999).

Solzhenitsyn, Alexander. "Live Not by Lies" (1974), http://www.orthodoxytoday.org/articles/SolhenitsynLies.php. Accessed 11 June 2017.

von Bremzen, Anya. *Mastering the Art of Soviet Cooking: A Memoir of Food and Longing* (New York: Crown, 2013).

Wasson, R. Gordon, and Valentina Pavlovna Wasson. *Mushrooms, Russia and History*, vol. 1 (New York: Pantheon, 1957).

List of Illustrations

Pyotr Vail and **Alexander Genis** were, as they noted, "geopolitically" Russian. Born citizens of the USSR—Vail in Riga, Latvia in 1949 and Genis in Ryazan, Russia in 1953—they emigrated in 1977 to New York, where they became writers, journalists, and radio broadcasters. Among their endeavors was a short-lived Russian-language newspaper for Soviet émigrés called *The New American*, which they launched with fellow émigré author Sergei Dovlatov. They also both worked for Radio Liberty, eventually hosting their own programs ("Heroes of Our Time" and "American Hour with Alexander Genis"). In 1995 Vail moved to Prague, where he headed the Russia desk and served as managing editor of Radio Free Europe/Radio Liberty until his death in 2009, while Genis remained in New York, where he lives to this day. Their writing partnership yielded two important books which make a significant contribution to the field of "everyday life studies," taking the reader back in time to participate in the 1960s Soviet experience (*The 60s. The World of Soviet People*) or 1980s émigré life (*Russian Cuisine in Exile*). Erudite and ethical, clever and kind, these two writers offer a view into the lives of displaced people. Their language and culture tied them to the vast empire which had ejected them, and their thoughtful and oft en entertaining engagement with politics and literature continues to attract readers across the globe today.